This book presented to

Sister Paula

Birthday

on the occasion of

Sr. Janita Ross

by

Jan, 27, 05

Date

Songs from a Mother's Heart

Meditations on the Psalms

Pamela J. Kennedy

CPH.
SAINT LOUIS

To my mother,
who taught me God is always there,
and to my mother-in-love, who raised my husband
to be a godly man.

Copyright © 1997 Concordia Publishing House
3558 S. Jefferson Avenue, St. Louis, MO 63118-3968
Manufactured in the United States of America.

———————————— Library of Congress Cataloging-in-Publication Data ————————————

Kennedy, Pamela, 1946-
    Songs from a mother's heart: meditations on the Psalms /Pamela J. Kennedy.
       p.   cm.
    ISBN 0-570-04891-5
    1. Bible. O.T. Psalms—Meditations. 2. Mothers—Prayer-books and devotions—
    English. I. Title.
    BS1430.4.K415   1997
    242'.6431--dc20   96-44101
                                                  CIP

3   4   5   6   7   8   9   10   06 05 04 03 02 01 00 99 98

∼ *Contents* ∼

As You Begin

This book is an interpretation of the psalmists' themes, filtered through the eyes and experiences of a mother. It is not intended to be a translation of the Psalms nor is it meant to be a paraphrase.

As I prayed over, studied, and meditated upon the beautiful writings of David, Asaph, Solomon, and others, I found patterns of hope, joy, and trust. Even in the most dire circumstances, God's faithfulness and steadfast love never failed. This is the message I long to share with mothers: God is as real and relevant today as He was when He first inspired the psalmists to write. His heart is touched by the fears of a young mother as much as it was by David's grief. He knows the frustrations, challenges, and triumphs mothers experience, just as He was acquainted with those of ancient shepherds, kings, and priests.

Take a few minutes before you begin reading to familiarize yourself with the contents of this book. Some meditations address issues you may be experiencing or have experienced. Some may reflect the situations of friends or family members. As you read each meditation, compare the thoughts with the psalm of the same number in your Bible. Even the meditations that do not directly apply to your life may lead you to new insights about God and His tremendous love for all mothers.

My hope is that mothers of all ages and at all stages will find in these psalms reasons to rest, rejoice, and rely on God—the Creator, Sustainer, Savior, and Sanctifier of mothers.

 *Pamela Kennedy*

Standing firm in a hostile society

O Lord, I know You want me to stay away
    from those who would lead me astray.
But their advice is so seductive.
They have so many studies
    and psychological treatises to give me,
    reasons and rhymes for raising my children.
Yet I see how they mock You, Father.
They have no guarantees—
    only theories couched in probabilities.
But You have given me promises.

Help me dig my roots deep into Your Word,
    to feel Your life pulsing through me.
I want to nourish my family
        with the fruit of Your choice,
    and reap a harvest ripe
        with Your wisdom and love.

All around I see families blasted apart
    by storms of selfishness, anger, and hate.
Or rotted from within
    by cancers of bitterness, despair, and apathy.
Father, guide me daily
    as I seek to mother as You desire.
Continue to watch over us as You promised
    and help our little family stand firm
    amid the domestic devastation around us.

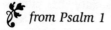 *from Psalm 1*

God's authority vs. human authority

All around us, Father, people are angry—
    angry at themselves, at one another, even at You!
They see Your Word as restrictive, narrow, binding,
    and their hatred builds.
In the name of freedom and choice, they pass laws
    trying to eliminate You from government, schools,
        even our homes.

Yet You have not changed, O God.
You still rule the universe and all in it.
How You must laugh at our feeble attempts
        to control life.
In Your wisdom You have placed all things
    under the authority of Your Son.
Those who defy You now will one day see
    their authority crumble into dust.

Remind me, Lord, that all wisdom comes from You.
Move me, as a mother, to seek Your will and wisdom.
Show me how to convey to my children,
        in words and actions,
    a holy balance of awe and rejoicing.
Help me set an example that influences them
    to honor You in daily life.
May our family find security not in institutions,
    which change and pass away,
    but in Your everlasting presence.

from Psalm 2

God's peace conquers fears

O Lord, I'm overwhelmed by the enemies of my peace—
    fear, doubt, despair.
I look at the situations I face with my children
    and I hear malevolent voices whisper:
        "God doesn't care."
        "He won't answer your prayers."
        "These problems aren't important to Him."

But then I recall Your past protection—
    the way You shielded me and held me up
        when I thought all was lost.

In my confusion and pain, I call to You again, Father,
    pouring out my mother's heart
        in tumbling words and aching sobs.
And once again You come to me
    with quiet, inexplicable peace
        that enfolds me like a comforting blanket.

In Your presence I find rest, despite my problems.
You are the strength that takes me through each day.
Yours is the courage I claim in every
    fear-filled confrontation.
Together, You and I not only face my enemies
    but vanquish them.
I find in You the deliverance I seek.
May I always remain
    in this place of blessing, Father.

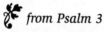 *from Psalm 3*

God's wisdom

O Father, I need Your answers today.
Yours are the responses that are true.
You are the source of the mercy and grace
    I need to meet the challenges I face.

I look at other families,
    other mothers, other children,
    and I see values that deny You, Lord.
People try to buy love with things,
    to fill their needs with money,
        to satisfy their hunger with power.
I know these are not the ways You choose,
    but sometimes the world's ways are very tempting.

Remind me that You have called me
    to be a different kind of mother;
        You don't want me to cave in to the
           "Everybody's doing it!" philosophy.
It's hard to face the anger of a self-righteous child
    and resist becoming angry in return.
I need Your calming touch
    to keep my heart pure and my mouth shut.
Father, these are the sacrifices You desire from me.

When others question the value
    of raising my children according to Your Word;
When they accuse me
    of having a view of life
        that's unrealistic and impractical,
          help me stand firm.

Let Your light and love shine
    through our family in such a way
        that others see the difference You make.
Make our joy in You so fulfilling
    that the world's goals
        of wealth and status and power
            become less and less beguiling.

Your peace is what we need
    in this crazy mixed-up world, Father.
You are the only one
    who can keep us safe in the midst of it.

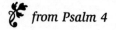 *from Psalm 4*

Prayer for a wayward child

Hear me as I come to You again, O Lord.
Every morning I cry out,
 bringing to You the desires of my heart.
I plead the case for my wayward child
 with sighs and tears,
  seeking Your wisdom,
   waiting expectantly for Your reply.
I know You see the path he has taken—
 the path of disobedience
 and self-centered arrogance.
I fear the consequences of his choice,
 yet I am powerless to turn him back.

Be patient with him, Father,
 and temper Your righteous judgment with mercy.
Give me grace to be submissive to Your will
 as You deal with this son I love so much.

Help me, O Lord, to see Your way clearly
 so that I, too, am not led astray.
It is tempting to follow the path of despair and anger,
 yet that is not the way You lead.
Give me, instead, a spirit of peace
 as I make my resting place with You.
Put a song on my lips and in my heart
 as I trust in Your protection for those You love.

Let this wandering one return
 to the blessings of obedience
  so he may once more enjoy
   the protection of Your loving-kindness.

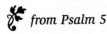 *from Psalm 5*

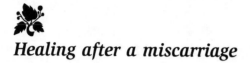

Healing after a miscarriage

O Lord, please don't give me any further anguish.
I need Your mercy like a desert needs the rain.
My heart is broken and even my body aches with grief.

I'm not sure I can go on, Father;
    how much longer must I bear the pain
        of losing this tiny one?

I should forget, move on, they say;
    it's just a miscarriage—
        so much better to lose it now than later.

But my tears won't stop falling;
    my dreams won't stop breaking—one by one.

In the night I see my never-born child,
    and I grieve for the times we will not share.

Well-intentioned friends, uncomfortable with my sorrow,
    try to wrest my attention from the loss.

But You, O God, You alone accept my tears,
    my prayers, my pleas for understanding.

You know my weakness and take pity on me,
    comforting me with Your love.

And in the quietness of Your presence, I will rest
    and gain strength for the journey out of grief.
Together with You,
    I will once more stand and face the morning.

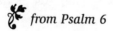 *from Psalm 6*

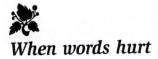

When words hurt

O Lord, my God, let me find refuge in You
 from those who seek to destroy me
 by slandering my child.
Their words cut and tear at our family,
 shredding the witness we seek to give.

Have I, in some way, fed the fire of gossip and hatred?
In my efforts to live my faith,
 have I become self-righteous or hypocritical—
 breeding resentment instead of love?
Keep me from the seductive twins of anger and revenge.
Cleanse me, O Father, that I might be used by You
 even in this situation.

You are the only one
 who can truly judge the heart, my Lord.
You know the straight path of righteousness
 when I see only a twisted trail of chaos and deceit.
Give me confidence to trust Your integrity,
 to cease my self-defense and rest in You.
For You, O God, know the way of all people.
You see the end from the beginning,
 and in Your time, truth will stand alone.
I will lay down my weapons of sarcasm and angry retorts.
I will give thanks for Your faithfulness,
 and trust You to bring Your righteousness to light.

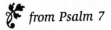 *from Psalm 7*

Wonder at a newborn

O Lord, my Lord,
    how mighty You are.
Your greatness cannot be contained in the heavens.

Yet as I look upon my newborn child,
    I see the imprint of Your fingers.
Here in my arms,
    the miracle of Your handiwork
        silences even the loudest skeptics.
Tiny arms and legs,
    stretching, wriggling,
        snuggle into my embrace.

How can I ever understand
    the intricate care You take with each of us?

This little one,
    freshly created by Your hand,
        will one day walk and talk,
            draw pictures,
        and solve algebraic equations.
Yet all that pales in comparison to Your plans for her.

Knit her life close to Your Son's.
    Guide her to choose His will above her own.
        Show her how to use her gifts to solve
            equations of the soul.

O God, my God,
    I am awestruck by Your glory and Your love,
        here, sleeping in my arms.

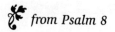 *from Psalm 8*

God's wisdom for mothers

I will praise You, O Lord, with all my heart.
I will tell my children of Your wonders.
I will be glad and rejoice in You.
I will sing praises to You.

When I choose to praise You,
  to rejoice despite my circumstances,
    my old enemies—fear and worry—flee.
I love to remember the many ways
  You have helped me in the past.
I recall the times You brought justice and mercy
  when I didn't know what to do.
When I felt oppressed and depressed,
  You were there.

So often, as a mother, I feel inadequate,
  unsure of what to do.
Is this child right, or is that one?
Do I favor one over the other?
Do I forgive one more easily
  and unwittingly breed resentment
    in the other's heart?

Because You always judge rightly,
  I come to You and seek Your wisdom, Lord.
You've promised to hear my cries,
  to grant me guidance.

Let me quietly reflect Your justice to my children,
  and in so doing, praise Your name.

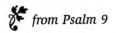 *from Psalm 9*

Prayer for abandoned children

Why is it, Lord, that You seem so far away?
I see children all around
    caught in poverty, mistreatment, and despair.
Abandoned by the ones who should care the most,
    they wander our city streets,
        lost and lonely.
My mother's heart breaks for these cast-off children,
    yet I feel powerless to help.

Evildoers prey on them,
    using them to satisfy appetites
    for degraded passions.
And no one seems able to stop this frightening tide.
Without shame, people mock You, Father,
    daring You to show Your face,
        taunting You to intervene.
They say, "God has forgotten.
    He is dead, gone, vanished in the mythic past."

But You do see, great Father of the fatherless.
Not one small sparrow falls outside Your care.
You hear the cries of the helpless;
    Your heart does bear their pain.

Despite the pride and arrogance of evildoers,
    Your will prevails.
You are the King who calls each to account.
You hear the prayers of Your little ones
    and will defend them with Your mighty hand.
Your day will dawn when children will no longer
    be terrified or alone.
And evildoers will see their power cease.

from Psalm 10

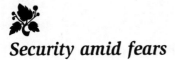

Security amid fears

You are my refuge, Lord.

People say to me: "You should move away from here.
    Take your children out of this place or that,
        keep them under lock and key, secure, protected.
    The world is not a safe place anymore."

Have they forgotten that You, O Lord, are God?
You are not some impotent monarch on an earthly throne,
    some petty politician with grandiose schemes.
You are King of heaven, King of earth.
You observe those who use their power
        to oppress others,
    and You alone know their eventual end.

In You is righteous judgment.
    You are the one who makes the upright triumph.

I cannot control the world in which my family dwells,
    but You are greater than the world,
        and in You we will find our dwelling place.

Lift our eyes to heaven as we seek Your grace
    and grant us the reward of seeing Jesus' face.

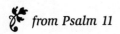 *from Psalm 11*

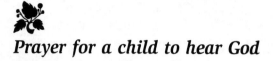

Prayer for a child to hear God

Help me, Lord.
Is there no one left who speaks the truth?

My children parrot slogans, hearsay, gossip
about how the world should be.
"Be first." "Get yours."
"Take it fast before it's gone."
"You have a right to own the best,
the most, the greatest."

Cliches born of greed and selfish opportunism
scream at them from morning until night,
promising treasures greater than gold.
Once bought, they turn to worthless, tarnished brass.

Your words are precious, Father,
pure and priceless,
shining with quiet dignity amid the gaudiness.

Help me make these words a reality to my children
as I listen to You and walk with You each day.

Then move my children to choose to hear reality—
to trade the world's cheap lies
for Your rich truth.

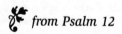 *from Psalm 12*

If a child dies

O Lord, have You forgotten me?
    I lift my voice to You
        and hear my words fall back like empty husks.

Where are You in this dark, dark place I'm living?
I'm like a blind person,
    lost and alone,
        wandering without direction.

My child has died, and I am so afraid.

Each day, all day long,
        my mind fights for sense or reason.
Each night, all night long,
        sorrow weights my heart with grief.

I'm losing in a battle for my sanity,
    and no one seems to understand my pain.

I need to hear Your voice, O Lord my God.
    Without Your light, I might as well be dead myself.

Those who mocked my faith must now feel vindicated,
    rejoicing to see my confidence in ruins.

Though I cannot hear You,
    I will trust You.
In the midst of this dark night,
    I will count on You for daybreak.
Though my song is in a new and minor key,
    I will sing on.

Now with all my safe religious trappings
        stripped away,
    as I stand before Your throne exposed, alone,
I see the only truth that is essential:
        You, Father, are a good and righteous God
        who saves the lost because of Your great love.

from Psalm 13

Teaching a child God "is"

All around I hear the voices
    of those professing wisdom.
They write books and teach classes and give speeches.
And while their subjects are varied,
    their theme is the same:

        There is no God.

My children hear them on television and in movies
    and listen to them in school
    and in the neighborhood.

And God, when You look down from heaven,
    Your heart must break.
You, who are a seeker of men and women,
    find few who seek You in return.
These same foolish people, trying so hard to deny You,
    are the very ones living in dread and fear,
        mourning the meaninglessness of life.

Help me teach my children well, Father.
    Use my lessons to impart to them the truth
        of Your presence
    in every aspect of life.
May they learn that salvation,
    not only in eternity, but in the present,
        originates and continues with You.
Give me the words and actions
    to equip them with wisdom—
    wisdom to stand against the tide of earthly opinion
    and shout with joyful affirmation:

God is!

 *from Psalm 14*

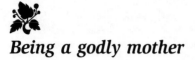

Being a godly mother

Lord, I want so much to be a good mother,
 to hear Your words, "Well done," when I face You.

How can I live up to Your expectations?

 to live in such a way that my children
  have no reason to blame me
   for their failures;

 to do the right thing
  instead of the easy thing;

 to speak the truth from my heart,
  not with arrogance but with love;

 to keep my speech sweet
  and free from gossip or slander;

 to treat others as I wish to be treated
  and never speak ill of another;

 to stand against evil
  and uphold the right;

 to keep my promises,
  even when doing so brings me pain;

 to willingly share with others
  from the riches You have given;

 to defend the innocent
  and those unable to defend themselves.

Only with Your power, O Lord,
    can I become the mother You desire.

Please help me stand with integrity,
    that I might please You, now and always,
        modeling to my sons and daughters,
            the example You have set for me
                through Christ.

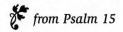 *from Psalm 15*

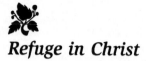

Refuge in Christ

Keep me secure, O God,
>for in You I take refuge.

I pray only to You and know
>that apart from You, I have nothing that is good.

There are some who claim to owe their success and joy
>to good fortune, luck, fate, or the stars.
Others give credit to hard work,
>good education, persistence, and good will.

But I know all I have comes from You,
>and I will not give praise to any other.
You have given me great blessings, Lord.
>My family, my home,
>>the very opportunity to be a mother—
>all come from Your abundant grace and love.

When I put You first,
>You guide my way,
>>give me wisdom, and set Your path before me.

Because You have granted me access to You
>through Your Son, I never need to be afraid.
Because of Your love, I can sing with gladness
>and tell my children of Your ways with confidence.

Because You have revealed the path of life,
>I know the peace of true security.
For on the day I leave my earthly home,
>I'll be at home with You eternally.

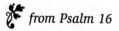 *from Psalm 16*

When a child challenges values

Lord, sometimes it's not easy to choose Your priorities
    when my children clamor to have and be and do
        the things that others cherish.

As a mother, I have tried to set guidelines
    in accordance with Your will,
        to walk in Your paths,
            to find pleasure in Your ways.
I experienced the delight of feeling secure
    in the center of Your love,
        under the shadow of Your wings.

It seemed so simple when my children were young,
    and they trusted me to lead them
        in safe and pleasant ways.

When did I become the enemy?
When did I begin to fear the anger
    in my children's voices?
Is it a rejection of You or me?
    or just a short-sighted focus on the here and now?

I cannot confront them, Father, without angry words
    and tearful accusations, making matters worse.
Would You rise up, O Lord,
    and fill my vision with Your grace?

Give me ears to hear Your wisdom before I speak
    so I reflect Your likeness to my family
        in such a way that worldly longings fade
            and Your priorities shine clear and true.

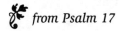 *from Psalm 17*

Thanks for a child's recovery

I love You, O Lord, my strength.
You are my rock, my fortress, my deliverer;
    You are the safe place in which I can hide.
You are the one who shields me and strengthens me.
    When I called to You—You who are worthy of praise—
        You saved me from my enemies.

When they told us our child had cancer,
    it was as if death had gripped us by the throat.
Disease became the destroyer—
    a vile enemy, coiling itself around my child,
        squeezing the life from her small body.
Everywhere I looked, darkness overwhelmed me.

In hopeless despair I called to You for help,
    not knowing what to say,
        only knowing You were there to hear me.

You did hear, and You came to stand beside us.
You entered into our pain and gathered us to Your side.

During the dark days of tests and diagnoses,
    You held us firm as the grim facts raged
        like stormy seas.
When my child's cries tore at my heart,
    You wrapped Your arms around me
        and soothed me with Your still small voice.
When medicines and radiation ravaged her frame
    and stole the vitality from her bones,
        You stood the night watch with us
            as we marked each breath and heartbeat.
Day after endless day, You never left us.
And in the midst of chaos,
    You brought a strange peace.

All the while, silent and unseen,
>   You fought a furious war with death, our enemy.
Slowly, almost imperceptibly,
>   Your victory became evident.
You reached down and drew us to Yourself
>   out of the pit of our distress.
The clammy grip of death was loosed,
>   and You lifted us to a place of hope and healing.

It was not because of our diligence, but Yours;
>   not because of our worth, but because of Your grace.
In a mystery deeper than our grief,
>   it was Your delight to heal our child.

What can I now say to sing Your praises?
O God, You have turned my darkness into light.
You have proved to me that with Your help,
>   I can face anything—
>   with You, no enemy is too great,
>   no barrier too high,
>   no battle too overwhelming.
Your ways and words are perfect.
There is no other God but You—
>   no Savior but Your Son, who is the Rock.

I sing my song of victory to You
>   for You have made me glad.
You have stretched out a future for my child
>   where there was none.
>   In bright and spacious places,
>   You will guide her feet.

I will not keep Your ways a secret
     but will shout with joy, "The Lord lives!
          Praises to His name! He is the God who saves!"

May I never cease to sing Your praises
     with a grateful heart.
And may I share Your loving-kindness
     with those who fear they struggle all alone.

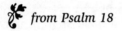 *from Psalm 18*

Wonder at God's order

I sat with my children in the quiet of the evening,
   and together we watched the sun disappear
      and waited for the first star's light.

As pink and gold painted the darkening sky,
   my youngest asked, "Is God an artist?"
"Yes," I replied, "the sky is His canvas
   and the light His palette of colors."

In silence we wondered at Your majesty,
   Your command of stars and moon and sun.
The order You have set in the heavens
   announces Your glory and wisdom to people everywhere.

When I see the trustworthiness of Your universe, O Lord,
   I know Your Word is faithful and Your ways true.
You have made Yourself knowable
   to even my little children, Father.

Help me to be diligent in showing them my trust in You.
Give me creative ways to help them understand
   that obedience brings joy,
      that seeking You brings wisdom,
         that honoring You brings integrity.

You are so precious to me, my Father,
   for You know my ways and love me still.
In Your mercy, You forgive my faults
   and restore me when I fall.

I want to be a woman who pleases You all my days.
May my speech and even my every thought
   be acceptable to You.

For You, O Lord, are my firm foundation now
and the one who leads me on into eternity
with Christ.

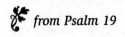 *from Psalm 19*

Sending a child to God for help

My child, as you stand before me
 with your tear-streaked face,
  it would be easy to soothe you with platitudes.
I could hold you in my arms and tell you,
 "Everything will work out.
  Tomorrow will be a brighter day."
But that would teach you only to trust me,
 to bring your problems to my feet for solving.
And even if I could give you solutions,
 they would only be temporary.
One day I will no longer be here to listen—
 you will leave or I will—
  and then where would you be?
So I will give you guidance
 that will last longer than we two.

Call upon the Lord in your distress
 and His name will protect you from your foes.
He will send you help in your time of need
 as you speak His name in faith.
He will give you the desires of your heart
 and cause your best plans to succeed.
When you fall, He will pick you up
 and set you on your path again.

I know this from my own experience;
 God saves and heals and lifts His children up.

There are those who won't believe in prayer.
They refuse to bow the knee or submit the will.
But you know better than they,
 for you know the truth.

So bring your heartache, my dear one, to His throne.
Pour out your pain and seek His healing grace.
He loves you with a love deeper than a mother's.
And in His hands, you will find strength to carry on.

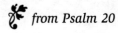 *from Psalm 20*

Prayer for a child's protection

O Lord, I rejoice in You.
You give me such joy through my children!

I longed to be a mother, to have little ones to raise,
    and You heard my prayers
    and gave these precious ones to me.

My dreams have been fulfilled
    in suntanned arms and legs,
        freckled noses, gales of laughter.

I watch them run and play, hair blowing in the wind,
    and my heart fills up with gladness.

What a picture of Your love these children are.

I ask for Your protection
        of their minds and hearts and bodies, Lord.
    There are many who would wish them harm.
The world is not an easy place for children, Father,
    even though I long to make it so for them.
Guard them with Your right hand,
    hold their enemies at bay
        and give them strength to conquer
            in Your name, O God.

I thank You for Your trust in giving me these little ones
    and seek Your strength to mother as I should
        so they will grow up singing songs to You
            and telling others of Your mighty love.

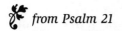 *from Psalm 21*

God's justice will prevail

My God, I feel forsaken.
 I cannot hear Your voice in the midst of my pain.
I cry out to You day after day,
 and in the night my prayers are endless.

My child faces his accusers,
 and they tear his reputation to shreds.
Their mockery and laughter
 wound like stabbing knives;
 their insults sting like lashes from a whip.

Did You feel like this
 when Your Son was punished for our wrongs?
Did You stand by and feel each word and injury
 cut into Your heart?
As You watched Him suffer,
 did You long to take the pain Yourself?

I know I cannot fight this battle for him,
 cannot even deflect an angry word,
 only observe and ache
 and lift my voice once more in prayer.

Deliver him, O Lord. Stay close
 and give Your strength and comfort to my child.
Rescue and defend him
 in the midst of this confusion and contempt.

I will praise You even in this present circumstance,
 with all its darkness and distress,
 for You refuse to hide Yourself from our pain
 but always hear and answer when we call.

All those who do wrong will one day
    face You with their guilt.
In Your time You will cause justice to prevail.

Let me rest in this assurance, Lord,
    that all will one day bow before Your throne
        in humble recognition of Your rule.
Your mercy and grace will blot out all injustice
    as generations sing Your praise.

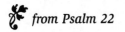 *from Psalm 22*

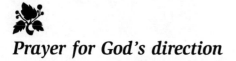

Prayer for God's direction

Lord, You are the one who cares for me.
    You provide me with everything I need
        to be a good mother.

You know that I will be exhausted sometimes,
    and for those times, You take me to quiet places
        where I can rest with You and be restored.

You show me through Your Word
    the way I should go
        so I will reflect with integrity
            the name of Your Son.

When doubts and fears,
    when the threat of danger, even death, surround me,
        I know You are there beside me.

I take comfort in knowing You will guide me
    with loving discipline when I need to be obedient,
        with Your power when I need strength to go on.

You will fill me with Your Holy Spirit
    so I am able to rejoice,
        even when surrounded by enemies of my peace.

I know that as I travel daily with You
    through this land called "Motherhood,"
        You will cover me with Your goodness and love.
And You and I will always be companions.

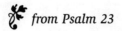 *from Psalm 23*

Prayer to trust God's leadership

The earth belongs to You, O Lord,
  and everything in it is Yours as well.
I need to remember Your ownership
  of all I look upon as mine:
    my home, my husband, my children, my faith.

For You created all things
  and established their place within Your universe.
I am only a tenant, a steward,
  of the things and relationships You have given me.

Help me not to worship what You have created
  and never to forget to worship You, the Creator.
Help me not to manage my family according
    to my desires and needs,
  but according to the truth of Your holy Word.

Let me hold my children loosely in Your love
  so they might feel Your hand upon them too.
And together may we experience Your rich blessing,
  the joy of one day seeing our Savior face to face.

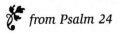 *from Psalm 24*

Prayer for God's instruction

O Lord, I lift my voice to You in prayer today
      because I have learned to trust You.
You understand how weak I am and love me still.

I need to see Your ways clearly, O God, my Father,
      because I have never walked this way before.
Other mothers seem to know instinctively
            what to do and say,
      but I am constantly in a quandary.
I have no special training for this job, Lord,
      and there is so little time to learn.

I remember the things I did as a child
      and my own mother's frustrations with me.
Mirrored now in my own children's faces,
      echoed in their voices,
            I see and hear my own selfish rebellion.

I know You are a loving teacher
      who gives upright instruction
            to Your wayward children.
Please help me, Father, to be a faithful student
            of Your Word,
      an obedient follower of Your Son.
Let my sons and daughters see Your justice
      reflected in my words and actions.
Give me the wisdom to stop and pray
      before I lose my temper and say hurtful things.
Forgive the selfish desire of my heart
      that longs to make my children extensions of myself,
            gaining prestige from their accomplishments
                  as if they were my own.

Teach me, Lord, to be like You:
    a patient teacher, an encouraging friend,
        a comforting and forgiving companion.

Day by day, let me find my model of mothering
    in the qualities of Your dear Son
        and in so doing,
    be the mother You would want me to be.

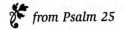 *from Psalm 25*

Letting an older child go

As my children prepare to strike out on their own,
    I feel uncertainty rise within me.

I have tried to follow Your commands
    before these children You entrusted to me, Lord.
I taught them Your words and showed them Your ways.
We took them to church each week
    and taught them to pray and sing Your praises.
I told them how You had helped me
    and encouraged them to trust You for everything.

Could I have done more?
Will they remember what they learned at home?
    Will their hearts hunger for Your Word?
        Will they seek You in prayer each day?
            Will they hold steadfast to their faith?

Forgive me, Lord, when I forget
    they are Your sons and daughters, not just mine.
All my teaching, training, tears
    are worthless without Your tender, loving care.
For You are the one who seeks and saves,
    the one who makes us hunger for Your Son,
        the one who draws us to Yourself.

Lord, give me grace to let them go with open arms,
    knowing You are there to hold them up.
I will give You praise for helping me do my best
    and will trust Your limitless love to do the rest.

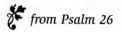 *from Psalm 26*

When a teenager rebels

"The LORD is my light and my salvation—
   whom shall I fear?
The LORD is the stronghold of my life—
   of whom shall I be afraid?"

When I say these holy words, O Lord,
   I feel Your confidence strengthening me.
      How I need that strength today, my Father.

When I imagined enemies assaulting me,
   I always pictured evil, dangerous people
      from somewhere else.
Never did I imagine they would come from my own home.
   Never did I dream my own children would turn on me!
"Adolescence is the time for testing," I've been told.
   "It's normal for children to be angry and rebel."

Sometimes it feels like an army is besieging me,
      like I'm in the midst of a battle,
   attacked on every side by arguments and tempers.
Every rule, each guideline, becomes a rallying point
   around which defiance swirls.
Tension is our constant companion,
   smirking at us from the corners
      of our children's mouths.
This is not what I imagined
   when I held my infants in my arms
      and dreamed of mothering them
         with tenderness and love!
Right now I just need You to keep me safe, O Lord—
   safe from my fears and frustrations,
      safe from the damage I might do
         by lashing out with hateful words.

Set me on a high and sturdy rock
   where I might see beyond this current fray.
Give me a vision of Your face, Father,
      so I might not forget the many times
         You have dealt with me in kindness,
            even when I was rebelling against You.

Keep me quiet with Your holy peace,
      even when these ones I love so dearly turn on me.

Teach me what You want me to learn
         through this experience
      that I might walk Your path well.

I know that whatever happens, You are always there.
      You never keep Your goodness from Your children.

I will wait with You to see my children grow
      and pray they will turn once more to You.

Please prepare my heart for each day that lies ahead
      and let me know the joy
         of standing in Your strength.

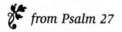 *from Psalm 27*

Joy in an unexpected pregnancy

Another baby, Lord?!
   I know this is a blessing from Your hand,
      but right now I am so tired
         and sick and overwhelmed.
Hear my prayers for strength and understanding, Father.

So many disregard Your gift of life
   and see it as a burden to be borne with resignation
      or one to be cast off, like unwanted baggage.
They show no regard for the miracle
   of a tiny growing child,
      the majesty of what You have begun
         and will, in Your perfect time, complete.

Despite my changing feelings, Lord, I will praise You.
You are the one to whom I go for strength.
You shield me from the moments
   of discouragement and despair.

Then I feel this new life move within me,
   and my heart leaps for joy!
      My lips sing a song of thanks
         for You have granted me the privilege
            of being a mother once again.

You are the one who changes doubts to peace,
   who takes my tired cries of complaint
      and turns them into hymns of praise.

Forgive my lack of faith, dear Jesus,
   for You are the shepherd who cares for me forever.

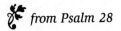 *from Psalm 28*

Prayer for a child's continued faith

O come, my children, and sing to the Lord with me!
    Sing of His mighty power and glory and strength.
Tell others of the wonderful things He has done.
    Lift up His name and worship Him always.

The voice of the Lord is more powerful than any other.
    When He speaks, you must listen, my little ones,
        for what He speaks is true.
He created the heavens, the seas,
    the crashing waves, the rolling thunder.
Light and dark obey His commands,
    and the earth itself answers when He calls.

But do not think He is so large
    that He cannot hear a little child like you.
For His greatness is as close as your very breath.

When you talk to Him in your prayers, He will listen.
    When you sing songs to Him,
        He will hear your every word.

Take time each day, my children, to speak to Jesus,
    for He is your Lord and King.

Your daddy and I will not always be with you,
    but Jesus will give you the strength you need.

And when you are afraid or uncertain or alone,
    His peace will hold you tighter than a hug.

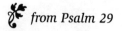 *from Psalm 29*

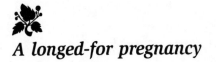

A longed-for pregnancy

I will praise Your name, O Lord,
    for You lifted me out of the depths of my grief.
You didn't leave me in my despair
    when I called on You for help.
You heard me and healed me, and in doing so,
    You have brought light to my darkness.

So long I desired to have a child, O Lord,
    to carry in my body the fruit of our love.
But year after year passed,
    and emptiness was all that filled my womb.
Through endless nights I cried out to You,
    yet now, in the bright joy of morning,
        my grief seems like a distant memory.

For You have answered our prayers,
    and eagerly we await the birth of our first child.
My lips now dare to form the word *motherhood,*
    to turn it round in my mouth like a delicious sweet,
        savoring every syllable with a smile.

My steps are lighter;
    my heart is lifted with a song of thanksgiving.
I cannot be silent in the midst of such jubilation.

How good You are to grant this deep desire of my heart.
    How natural it seems to sing Your praises
        to all I meet.
For You took mercy on me, Father,
    and in Your grace, have placed a tiny new life
        within my care.

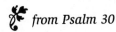 *from Psalm 30*

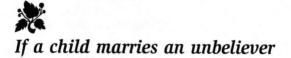

If a child marries an unbeliever

In You, O Lord, I have taken refuge;
    I cannot speak of my pain to others.

My child has fallen in love
    with someone who does not love You, my Savior,
        and my heart aches
            for the distress I see ahead.
I know that only You can do the work
    that changes minds and hearts
        and accomplishes the miracle of obedient faith.

Into Your hands I commit my spirit;
    I pray for Your redemptive power, O Lord.
Keep my demeanor meek and my words healing.
    Give me grace to speak
        with wisdom cloaked in love.
Open my child's eyes, O Lord,
    to see with clarity the path he has chosen.

I look around and see our friends and neighbors
    in their disapproval,
        shaking their heads and wagging their tongues.
Even those I have known for years avoid me,
    acting as if our family has defected from the faith.
Their rejection hurts,
    yet it is not my main concern,
        for I trust You, O Lord.
I say, "You are my God.
    My times are in Your capable and loving hands,
        and I know You bring deliverance."

But would You look with mercy upon my child?
  Give him the courage to stand by his convictions
    in the face of temptation.
Turn the heart of his beloved to You, dear Lord,
  that she might see You as her Savior too.

I pray for them to be united in their faith,
  to have a marriage bound in body, soul, and spirit
    with Your precious Son.

I know my prayer isn't too difficult for You to answer.
I will be strong, take heart, and hope in You.

from Psalm 31

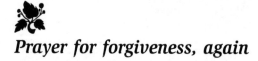

Prayer for forgiveness, again

O Lord, I need Your blessed forgiveness today.
 I long to feel new and clean again,
  to have the opportunity to start over,
   to try again to be the mother You desire.

I seem to have such good intentions,
 then I fall into the same old habits.
I speak roughly when I should be loving.
 My anger rises over trivial irritations.
  I jump to conclusions
   before listening to explanations.

Sometimes my expectations are too high
 for little hands to meet,
  my instructions too complicated
   for childish minds to grasp.

Then, frustrated, I place the blame
 at their feet, not mine.

I recall the times You have had to teach me, Lord,
 the same lessons time and time again.
You are so patient and so loving as You forgive
 my failures.

Forgive again my selfish shortness of temper,
 my impatient words,
  my critical looks and gestures.

Give me a teachable heart,
 a childlike faith that trusts You
  with total confidence.
Instruct me in the way I should go as a mother.
 Counsel and watch over me.

Make me sensitive to every urging of Your Spirit, Lord,
   so that my children see Your influence in my life.

Thank You for allowing me to come to You when I fail.
Thank You for Your cleansing, healing power
   when I'm torn by sin.
Thank You for this new opportunity for obedience.

I praise You for Your unfailing love
   that lifts me like a joyful song
      and gives me gladness as I face tomorrow
         filled with hope, not guilt or sorrow.

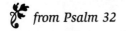 *from Psalm 32*

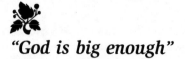

"God is big enough"

O Lord, I sing joyfully of Your greatness and love.
    For You are faithful, and every word You speak is true.

Tonight I laughed as I tucked my little son into bed.
    "How big is God?" he asked.
        "Bigger than anything!" I said.
    "Bigger than Daddy?"
        "Much bigger."
    "Bigger than Batman?"
        "Oh, yes."
    "Than Superman?"
        "Yes indeed!"
    "Then just how big is He?" he questioned,
        eyes wide in wonder.

"Big enough to speak and make the stars obey.
    Strong enough to push the waters of the deepest sea.
    Brave enough to beat the greatest armies.
    Wise enough to know the thoughts of everyone.
    Loving enough to hold the hand of a little boy
        who trusts in Him."

My son smiled then and snuggled under his covers.
    "Mmmm," he sighed with a sleepy voice,
        "then I guess He's big enough."

I brushed his cheek with my fingertips
    and gently kissed his nose.

How great You are, O loving Father,
    to care for us so tenderly.

May my son learn to trust Your holy name,
　　to place his hope in You,
　　　　to know with every certainty
　　　　　　that You are always "big enough."

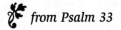 *from Psalm 33*

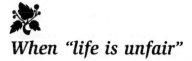

When "life is unfair"

O Lord, my child came home today,
    threw her school books down,
        and, with a teenager's righteous indignation,
           declared, "Life is just not fair!"
Then she recited her litany of despair,
    proof from the halls of high school
        that her claim is true.

Father, give me the wisdom of Your Spirit,
    the tenderness of Your Son,
        to point her to the truth about life and You.
Help me share with her how You are always there
    for those who seek You,
        that those who cry to You do find justice.
Open her eyes to see the angels
    You set around us as protection,
        the goodness You lavish upon us,
           the blessings with which You shower us.

Come, my daughter, and listen to what I say:
    You must be about God's business.
    You must be a speaker of truth,
        a seeker of peace, a worker of justice.
For God is looking for men and women
    who long for righteousness.

Those who prosper now through evil means,
    those who seem to get away with murder,
        will one day see their troubles
           return to them.

Those who are victims of unfairness now
　　will be vindicated by the Lord.
Have no fear. He hears every cry,
　　every prayer, every broken heart.

The Lord is the one
　　who will break down the strength of evildoers.
And it is He who will lift up those who suffer.

It is good to remember that
　　　although life is often unfair,
　　the God we serve is always just.
Those who go to Him for help will never be condemned.

from Psalm 34

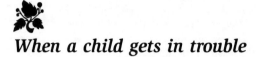

When a child gets in trouble

Lord, You need to fight this battle for me.
>I'm frustrated and confused and hurt at every turn.

When the phone call came
>and we learned of his actions,
>>I was incredulous!
How could this be?
>Where had we gone wrong?
>>Why had we failed to see this trouble coming?
I went to my friends for prayer and support,
>but I found only condemnation!
I needed understanding and help,
>but I received looks that accused
>>and words that stung.

"You should have been more lenient with him,
>not so restrictive and narrow."

"You should have set firmer limits—
>to spare the rod just spoils the child!"

And beneath their words of advice
>I could hear the gloating,
>>the self-assured confidence,
>>that *their* child would never behave as mine.
It's as if they rejoice in my pain,
>confirming their own success with my failure.

I know I shouldn't allow them to shake my faith, Lord,
>but I hear their whispered conversations,
>>see their covert glances,
>>>and my face burns with anger and shame.

O Lord, I know You see this too.
 Stay close to me during this time, Father.
Help me focus on You, not them.
 Remind me to let You be my vindication.
Help me to seek Your face,
 to follow Your directions in obedience.
Teach me the lessons You want me to learn
Free me from the bitterness that tempts me
 so I can help my wayward child.
Teach me to praise You not only when things go well
 and I stand in the midst of friends
 but in the lonely times when they turn away
 and I stand alone with You.

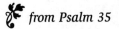 *from Psalm 35*

Prayer for a sleeping child

Tonight, my Father,
    I tiptoed in to watch my children sleep.
Curled in quilts and pillows,
    they sighed in dreams too deep for words.
Tiny arms and legs
    flung with abandon around teddy bears and bunnies.
So safe, so peaceful,
        so innocent of all that lies beyond our home.

Even as I reveled in their quietness,
    I could hear the clamoring din that threatens.
The world, sitting outside our door like a hungry lion,
      waits to attack and tear these little ones apart
        with doubt and prejudice and hate.

But I will look to You to do what I cannot.
    Your love reaches higher than my fears, O Lord.
Your righteousness is a mountain mightier
      than my worried thoughts.
    Your justice is deeper than my sea of concerns.
How priceless is Your unfailing love!

My children will go out into the world,
    but they will never go without
      the nourishment of Your Word
    or the life-giving river of living water
      found in Your Son.

Protect these little ones from the proud and the wicked.
May the light they live by be Your light
      and the truth they seek Yours.

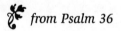 *from Psalm 36*

When a child is treated unfairly

I watch my son walk home from school
   and see the familiar slump of his shoulders.
His steps are slow,
   and listlessly, he kicks a rock along before him.
I open the door, and he looks up.
   Muddy tears smudge his cheeks,
      and I know he has had a rough time again.

O Father, how can I explain why children are unkind
   to those who aren't as fast
      or as bright
         or as beautiful as they?

I gather up the books where they've been dropped
   and follow my unhappy child into the kitchen.
We pour two glasses of milk and sit together.
   He looks at me, those same questions in his eyes.

"Mom, why do the kids tease me?
   Why won't they just be my friends?
      Why don't they want to play with me?"

My heart aches with the longing to take away his pain,
   to spare him the disappointment he feels,
      to make the world a different place for him.
Silently, I pray for wisdom,
   and You, as always, answer with Your words of life.

"Don't be jealous of those who seem to be popular.
   They won't always be the ones in charge.
Trust in the Lord. Ask Him to help you do what's right.
   He knows what You want and the right ways to get it.
Trust Jesus to bring you good friends,
   to help you get along,
      and He will surprise you with what He can do.

Keep from becoming angry and bitter
    and don't try to be mean in return.
Before long, those who are unkind,
        those who constantly hurt others,
            will find they are the ones who are hurting.
They will learn there is no happiness
        in making others sad,
            there is no joy in causing others pain.

When you ask Jesus to help you do what's right
    and act with care and kindness,
        He gives you a peace no one can steal.
God sees what is happening,
    and He knows how hard it is for you, my child.
He loves those who love His ways,
    and He will never take His love away from you."

I know these words are true, my Father.
But I have lived long enough to see
    how mighty people often have the greatest falls,
        how fame is fleeting
            and power like a passing wind.

My son is young and only sees the here and now.

Protect him from the lifelong sting of childhood hurts.
    Strengthen his young faith through Your dear Son.

You are my stronghold, Lord,
    the one who helps me and my children
        when the hurts of life seem hard to bear.
You are the one who takes our hands
    and walks us through this life into the next.

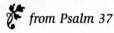 *from Psalm 37*

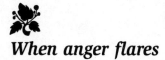

When anger flares

O Lord, I need Your forgiveness.
    I have wounded my child with my temper,
        and my words have cut deep as a knife.

How many times have I tried to be calm,
    yet the habits of a lifetime propel me
        into turbulent waters.
The very things I vowed never to do,
    I do, not once but over and over again.
Sometimes I feel I should never have had children,
    for often I am more a child than they.
They look to me for kindness and respect,
    and in my selfish anger, I so easily put them down.

When I confess, You so graciously forgive,
    but soon I go my own way and sin once more.
Will I ever be the mother You want me to be,
    showing my children the pure love of Christ?

You know my heart's desire—
    to raise my little ones as You teach,
        to bring them up to love You, Lord.
But my strength fails me.

I cry to You for forgiveness once more, my Savior.
    Hold me firm so I won't slip again.
        Help me submit my emotions to Your control.
Stay close beside me, Lord,
    so I will sense Your presence every moment.
Help me filter my words and actions
    through the prism of Your endless love.

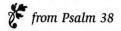 *from Psalm 38*

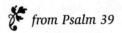

Focusing on important details

Today I met with lots of other mothers, Lord.
    I meant to keep my mouth shut and listen.
But the longer I listened to their stories,
    to their complaints, to their grievances,
        the more upset I became.
They expend so much energy
    debating things with no eternal value—
        arguing about issues that will soon disappear:
What color to paint the cafeteria: 60 minutes.
How many science and math kits to buy: 30 minutes.
Class field trips: Ran out of time.

In the hallways, I hear profanity and cruel taunts.
    On the playgrounds, bullies overpower timid children.
        Teachers struggle with disrespect
            from parents and students alike.

When will we wake up and see that life
    is just a brief encounter with space and time?
When will our priorities be focused on minds and hearts
    instead of property and fixtures?

Our days on earth are numbered by Your will, O Lord.
Help us spend our allotted time
    doing things that matter.
When I stand before You, Father,
    let me present as a gift to You
        the lives touched in Your name—
            not the color of the cafeteria wall.

from Psalm 39

Called to work with children

Lord, I have waited prayerfully
    for You to show me the place of service
        You have prepared for me.
My children are finally in school,
    and I have time to devote to serving You
        in the church.

I asked You for direction, anxious to see
    what place You had ready for me to fill.
Then the call came,
    and it was not at all what I had planned.

Nursery coordinator?
    Are You playing some kind of joke, Lord?
Don't You think I've had enough
    of bottles, bibs, and diapers to last a lifetime?
I was thinking more of working with adults
    or maybe teens—at least someone who could converse!

As I questioned Your good judgment,
    I heard that still small voice probing my motives.
"Who better than a mother to tend My little lambs?
    Who knows better the concerns of worried parents
        as they leave a child?"

"But I'll work hard and study
        to prepare exciting lessons
    that challenge young people
        to give their lives to You!" I replied.

"And you'll be praised instead of Me,"
    You answered me, Lord.

In my shame, I knew that You were right.
    You do not want the sacrifice and offerings
        of pride
    but a willing body, mind, and spirit.

I desire to do Your will, O God.
    Forgive my selfishness,
        which seeks my own interests instead.
Give me Your grace to care for these little ones
    with joy and gladness.
Help me use the things You've taught me
    as I touch these children with Your love.
Make this their first step on the path of faith.

from Psalm 40

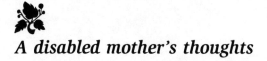

A disabled mother's thoughts

O Lord, I sit and watch my children play,
    fighting down thoughts of other mothers
    who can run races with their children,
        wrestle with them in the grass,
            and push them higher, higher in a swing.
My eyes stray to my useless legs
    and this chair that frees and binds me both at once.

I know You are my strength and hope,
        that You have blessed me in so many ways,
    yet my old adversaries—envy and despair—taunt me.
"If God loves you, why has He allowed this pain?"
"Look at other women. They don't suffer so."
And deep within my heart, doubting voices rise again,
    "If you only had enough faith, God would heal you."
        "Is there some secret sin you're hiding?"
            "Trust, just trust, and you'll walk again."

Even my best friends tire of the inconvenience
    of dealing with my uncooperative limbs.
I see the burden I have become to them.

I fear my children will resent a mother
    with limited abilities and strength
        and, in their disappointment, turn away.

But You, dear Jesus, know what it's like
    to deal with this kind of pain.
You limited Yourself willingly
    when You came to die for me.
You set aside Your heavenly strength
    that I might be empowered for eternity.

Forgive me for my complaining heart
that focuses on what I do not have
and overlooks the blessings You have given:
healthy children, home, family, and friends.

One day I'll walk with You, and even run,
but now I'll sing Your praises from this chair.
"Praise be the Lord, the God of all the ages,
let all that is within me praise His name."

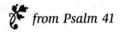 *from Psalm 41*

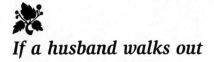

If a husband walks out

"As the deer pants for streams of water,
    so my soul pants for You, O God.
My soul thirsts for God, for the living God."

I have poured out my heart to You in tears;
    day and night, I cry to You, O Lord.
I cannot eat. I cannot think. I cannot even pray,
    except to say Your name.

I remember how we used to go to church—
    the perfect family, walking side by side.
Handsome father, mother, son, and daughter—
    a cover picture for the church directory.

Now he says he wants out;
    he feels trapped, engulfed by all our needs,
        overwhelmed by the responsibility.
And I am terrified of being left alone—
    alone to raise two little children by myself.

Put your hope in God.
    Rely on Him. Praise His name,
        the one who never changes or deserts you.

How can I face the future
    with my dreams in shreds around my feet?
How can I face my family,
    my church, my friends, my children
        when they ask where Daddy is?

Remember the one who walks beside you,
  the one who faces each day with you,
    the one who brought you this far
      and will take you on from here.

How could I be so blind to his unhappiness,
  so oblivious to his discontent?
How have I failed as a wife and mother
  that he can now cast me off so easily?

Remember that each is free to choose.
  Each must bear responsibility for his own sin.
But the Lord is greater than your pain.
  He is the one who saves despite the situation.

O God, I am exhausted by my grief,
  anguished by the pain within my heart.

Put your hope in Jesus, the Christ,
  your Savior and your God.
He will give you rest.

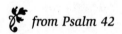 *from Psalm 42*

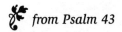

Being a light to the nation

O God, I read the papers
    and watch the nightly news
    and listen to the radio
  and wonder what in the world is going on!

Is this country safe for my children
    if the freedom that we cherish is denied
        to anyone who differs with the proper views?

I pray for my family and for myself:
    Show us how to bring Your light to the darkness.
    Move us to close our nation's gaping wounds.
    Teach us to offer hope for hopelessness,
        kindness for cruelty,
            peace for war.
Keep us faithful to the task before us, Lord.
    Help us guide others to the mercy of Your Son
        and build Your kingdom in our hurting world.

We place our hope in You
    and praise You, Lord,
        for nothing is too difficult for You.

from Psalm 43

Thanks for a heritage of faith

What a heritage we have, O God.
Generations before us have experienced Your love,
    and passed that knowledge to us.
Great-great-grandfathers and grandmothers
    lived and prayed and sang their hymns to You.
Now I enjoy that rich legacy and acknowledge
    the deep responsibility to pass it on once more.

Help me share Your truth with my children.
May they clearly see You
    and feel Your presence in their hearts.
Let me use words and actions that lift You up
    as the one who conquers all by Your holy name.
Enable me to teach my children
    that only You bring lasting victory.

The world offers so many false heroes
    who promise quick success or easy remedies.
May my children cherish the priceless gift of triumph
        that's theirs through Your dear Son's death
    and treasure all the more the faith
        You have given them.

When they fear defeat,
        when others taunt their faith
            or threaten to destroy them,
        then, O God, remind them how You fought
            for Abraham, Isaac, and Jacob
    and how You still redeem Your sons and daughters.
Rise up and help them in their time of need.
    Let them know the force of Your unfailing love.

from Psalm 44

When a daughter marries

O Father, I look at my daughter in her wedding dress
    and wonder at the passage of so many years.
Today she walks a narrow path
    that takes her from our home to her own.
Bless her and keep her close, O Lord.
Give her strength and courage, grace and wit
    to face the days You have stretched before her.

This young man standing before the congregation,
    brave and earnest in his rented clothes,
        will be a husband in a few short minutes.
Fill him with truth, humility, and righteousness, God.
Go before him as he faces all that lies ahead.
Help him seek wisdom as he begins each day
    and dedicate his plans to Your direction.

Music swells as friends and family
    rise to greet the bride.
My heart fills with memories
    as I see her smile at her father and take his arm.
Was it so long ago she chased a puppy in the sun
    or cried her heart out over adolescent dreams?
A woman now, confident and beautiful,
    she steps down the aisle.
I praise You, Father, for entrusting her to us,

These two will travel on together now,
    united by their vows and Your great love.
May they establish their home as Your home
    and learn the joy and gladness of Your peace.

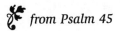 *from Psalm 45*

God is the family's strength

O God, how I praise You
    for being the strength in our family.
I know that whatever threatens us—
    troubles from without or within our home—
        I need not fear. You are with us.

There is a peace that keeps us safe
    in the midst of any storm.
It is the peace of Your Son, Jesus,
    who dwells within our hearts.
There is a strength that empowers us
    in the midst of any trial.
It is the strength of Your Holy Spirit,
    who flows with life-giving streams within our souls.

You are our help in the morning
    and when the night is dark around us.
You are our protection when enemies roar against us,
    or when they whisper insidious accusations.

Nothing can prevail against Your loving power.
No one can be victorious over You.

In the still, silent splendor of Your presence, Lord,
    I hear You speak: "Child, know that I am God."

 *from Psalm 46*

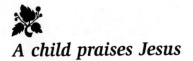

A child praises Jesus

Chubby hands clap and
    infant voices lisp Your praises, Jesus.
Laughter rises like sweet perfume
    as I sing together with my children
        alleluias to Your name.

How great You are
    to listen to the praise of children.
How marvelous is Your grace
    to bless our home with these young lives.

These little ones are the inheritance
    You have granted us.
Theirs is the faith which we now build.

Sing to the Lord, my children, sing forever.
    Sing to the Lamb for He is a mighty king.

Heaven and earth belong to Him now and always.
    He is the one who reigns forevermore.

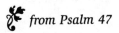 *from Psalm 47*

Prayer for the home

You are great, O Lord, and worthy of our praise.
   In our family, we will teach our children
      of Your beauty and Your holiness.

May I, as a mother, lean on Your strength
      to guide my children
   and to be a loving and supportive wife.

When the forces around us threaten our unity
   or assault our values and morality,
      give us wisdom to stand
         in the integrity of Your Word.

You are the security we seek in a world
   as changing and unpredictable as a stormy sea.
Morning and evening we meditate
   on Your love revealed through sacred writing
      and answered prayer.

You have never failed to deal with us righteously,
   and Your judgments are good and true.
Within our home, Yours is the place of honor.
We rejoice in Your presence in our hearts and lives.

Let our home shine as a place of love and hope
   for the needy and hopeless around us.
Give us courage to tell of Your mighty works
      to all we meet
   so others may know You and welcome You
      as their Savior and Guide.

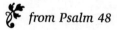 *from Psalm 48*

Avoiding materialism

O listen, my children,
    you who see and desire
        every new item on the market;
    you who envy your friends' designer clothes
        and name-brand shoes
        and robots that talk
        and dolls that walk;
    you who believe the advertisers' seductive
        promises of popularity
            if you get rid of your pimples
            or straighten your curly hair;
    you who rush to the shrine of the shopping mall
        and frantically search for things
        to fill your hearts' deepest longings;
    this is the lesson I would have you learn,
        the truth that you need to know:

Nothing you buy brings joy that lasts.
A person who loves you for what you own
    won't be a friend who will stand beside you.

It is a hard lesson but a true one.
In the end, all we have—
    our homes, our cars, our clothes, our toys—
        will be left behind.

What do you have, my daughter, my son,
    what do you have that will last?

Only God is everlasting,
    and what you give Him, He keeps forever.
Invest your time and talents for His kingdom.
    Entrust your very heart and mind to Him.

People can steal your things,
    ruin your clothes,
        damage your room,
            or break your favorite toys.
But no one can ever steal you from the Lord.
    He will always keep you in His care.

from Psalm 49

Recognizing God's riches for mothers

So often, God, I bargain with You.
 "If You will just do this ...,"
  and small, empty promises escape my lips.
I think I can somehow influence You to do my will,
 getting our roles all topsy-turvy.

Then You remind me of Your majesty,
 how You speak and the sun rises at Your voice,
  how moons and stars and planets
   rush to do Your will.

Forgive me, Father,
 for trying to contain You
  in my tiny sphere of influence.
Forgive me, Father,
 for acting like a spoiled, selfish child.

I see the many blessings You have given—
 a good husband, healthy children, a home.
Why do I always feel dissatisfied,
 wanting something more, some added blessing,
  assuming it will fill the emptiness I feel?

Is it because I have forgotten my heritage in You?
Have I failed to claim the wealth
  You give me in Your Son
or overlooked the riches of Your grace?

Forgive me when I focus on this world and its agenda,
 forgetting I am a citizen of another realm.
Let me give thanks to You for Your mercy
 and turn my eyes upon Your all-sufficiency.

Let me sing with joy
    hymns of thanksgiving
        and raise Your name
            before my family with praise.

Rescue me from the sinking sand of selfishness
    and set me on the rock of Your greatness
        that I might honor You
            and live out Your salvation every day.

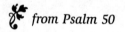 *from Psalm 50*

Asking God for cleansing

I need Your mercy, O God.
　　Only You have the loving compassion
　　　　to forgive me and help me begin again.

I long to feel clean and fresh once more,
　　to start over, freed from the guilt of my sin.

I see what I have done
　　and am filled with self-loathing.
It is You I have betrayed
　　by willfully disobeying Your Word,
　　by doing and saying those things
　　　　that disgrace Your holy name.

You have every right to cast me away
　　for I knew the way to go
　　　　and chose another path.

I cast myself on Your mercy, Jesus,
　　and come before You broken and contrite.

If You wash away my sin,
　　I will be clean once more.

If You accept my offering of sorrowful repentance,
　　I will know joy again.

Strip away my sin
　　and clothe me in Your righteousness.
Purge my heart
　　and fill it with Your Holy Spirit's purity.

With Your enabling power,
    I will turn from my sin
        and stand in the resurrection power
        of You, my Savior.

Let me speak once more for You, O God,
    and share Your grace with family and friends,
        cleansed from the stain of my rebelliousness.

I bring You nothing but my broken heart
    and ask for nothing but Your healing, Lord.
True forgiveness comes only by Your grace.
    Only in Your mercy is there hope.

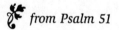 *from Psalm 51*

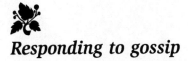

Responding to gossip

I have just overheard some gossip, Lord,
    and I am filled with anger.
Cruel words and untrue accusations
    have been launched against me,
        and I long to hurl them back.

Tongues, sharp as razors,
    slash and cut a reputation
        I have worked years to build.
Uncontested rumor dashes eagerly from place to place,
    anxious to spread its poison far and wide.

In my hurt, I would so quickly hurt another,
    feeling justified and pleased to do the harm.
Then I hear my voice instructing my children,
    reminding them to let You fight their battles.

It is so easy to teach others of Your ways,
    yet difficult to apply the lesson to myself.

Help me remember that my vengeance
        only brings destruction
    and my urge to get even
        will only drag me down.

I am Your child, and You will be my stronghold.
    I will be still and watch You set things right.
Planted in Your garden,
        I cannot be uprooted nor displaced,
    and Your careful tending will bring sweet fruit.

Make this experience a time of learning, Lord,
    a time to know Your love in new and different ways.
Help my children see that trusting You
    is the best defense against slander.
For You know what it is to be accused unjustly,
    and You know what it is to rise again!

🌿 *from Psalm 52*

Explaining evil in the world

My children and I watched the pictures
    as they played across the television screen.
Mothers, fathers, children
    running from the armies that would harm them.
Faces gripped with fear and streaked with tears
    screamed helplessly before us.
Hopelessness and terror ran beside them,
    chasing, hunting down the frightened prey.

Then my child, with tears in her own eyes,
    asked the question old as time itself:
        "Why doesn't God do something?"

How do I explain the puzzle of why we choose sin
    when alternatives like love and peace
        would end our pain?
How can I share the grim reality of chosen death
    when life is offered freely from Your hand, O Lord?
When evil people murder and deny their guilt,
    how do I teach my children to respect the truth?

Help me affirm Your sovereign majesty
    and draw my children closer to Your Son.
For in the final battle, only He stands
    righteous and victorious over wrong.
Those who triumph now by shameful acts of sin
    will one day kneel in abject sorrow at Your throne.

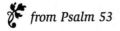 *from Psalm 53*

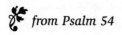

A child facing rejection because of faith

I taught my son to speak up
    when his faith was tried,
  and trustingly he took me at my word.
Today at school he made a point of speaking up.
    Now he faces teasing and rebuke.

How hard it is to see my child hurting, Lord,
    suffering for his faith at this young age.
Use this rejection to make him stronger,
    wiser in his faith.

My mother's heart would gather him in,
    hold him tightly,
    try desperately to erase his pain,
        but You have said this is the path of blessing,
          the way he will come to see Your face.

Your arms are the ones he needs to feel right now,
    strengthening and helping him stand.
Give me the courage to let him learn the joy
    of speaking Your truth, even when it is rejected.

Help me teach him even now to praise Your name
    and focus on Your grace, not his pain.

from Psalm 54

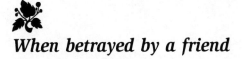

When betrayed by a friend

Listen to my prayer, dear Jesus.
I need to know You hear and answer me.
    I'm confused and hurt and don't know where to turn.

My mind is tangled with fear and despair,
    and all I want to do is run away and hide.
But how can I escape my own anguish?
    Where can I go to get away from my own thoughts?

My best friend has betrayed me,
    and I still can't comprehend the reason why.
We shared so many things throughout the years:
    dreams and heartaches,
        advice and recipes,
            joys and sorrows.
We helped each other through our pregnancies,
    first babies, teething, chicken pox, preschool—
        encouraging, cajoling, praying together.

It would be easy to bear hatred from an enemy,
    but to see a sister turn her back and walk away
        brings sharp, unrelenting pain.
All day long I think of conversations we have had,
    and in the night, her words of anger sting my heart.

Sleep eludes me.
    Bitter tears fall,
        and my throat aches with stifled sobs.

Only You, who knew the pain of betrayal so well,
    only You can understand and heal my heart.
I cast my cares on You, my Savior,
    and seek Your sustenance once more.

I do not know how this will end for us,
    or when or if this break will finally mend,
  but I know You, and in Your strength I will abide,
    and trust in You to bring me through it, Lord.

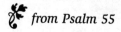 *from Psalm 55*

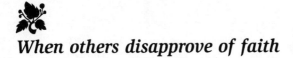

When others disapprove of faith

The last thing I wanted to be, Lord, was an activist!
    I just saw a wrong and spoke up
        because I could not stand by
           and tolerate the sin any longer.

Now I am featured on the front page of the paper,
        quoted and misquoted,
           characterized, labeled, and stereotyped—
this week's topic of conversation and debate.

My children wonder what the fuss is all about.
    Is Mommy famous or a criminal?
    Why are all the people calling on the phone?

At the market, I see people stop and whisper.
    Is the price of oranges
        or my presence what stirs their interest so?
Am I becoming paranoid
    or just more wise to worldly ways?

It seemed so clear and plain
    when I spoke out,
        but now words I don't recognize
           are said to be my own.
Things are neither clear nor plain at all.

O Jesus, You know what my motives were.
    You understand the words I said
        and why I spoke as I did.
You know, dear Lord, just what it feels like
    to have your statements twisted,
        sifted, bent, and torn,
        then tossed back at you, practically unrecognizable.

I believe that You can bring about good,
 even from this ugly situation.
I trust You
 and Your Word, which never changes.
What can others do to me
 if I am in Your hands?

I will give thanks to You,
 for You have saved my soul,
  and in Your grace,
   You show me how to walk in the light.

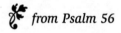 *from Psalm 56*

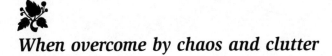

When overcome by chaos and clutter

Have mercy on me, O God,
    have mercy on me,
        for in You I am safe and protected.

I need to get away to a quiet place,
    to find some moments of solitude.

I feel like I am sinking in a sea of needs,
    overwhelmed by the demands on my time.
Crying babies, messy rooms,
    runny noses and dirty diapers,
        meals and dishes and dust
            fill my minutes, hours, and days.

Somewhere in the middle of it all,
    I think I lost myself.
        I can't escape all the demands,
            but I can't meet them either.

Could You show me Yourself in the midst of my mess, Jesus?
Would You illuminate me with Your love and faithfulness?

I know You are higher than the piles of laundry,
    deeper than the ground-in dirt.
Your song is louder than a baby's cry,
    and Your love more insistent than a whining child.

I just feel trapped right now, caught
    in mind and body by motherhood's unbreakable nets.

Fix my heart on You, my Lord.
Open my ears to the music of Your Spirit within me.

Strengthen my grip on Your vision for my life
    so I can see the mundane
        through the lens of eternity.
This hectic time will pass
      and children will too soon be gone,
    and quiet, peaceful days will fill my weeks.

I will thank You even in the chaos of my world today
    and sing Your praises louder than the din around me.
Your love cannot be covered up with clutter, God,
    for You are greater than whatever hems me in.

Change my focus to Your focus
    and set my mind on finding joy in little things.
Help me search for times when You and I can talk
    even if it's over sinks of dirty pans.

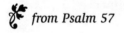 *from Psalm 57*

When a child's feelings are hurt

Today I walked my daughter to the park.
As I sat and read a book,
  I heard her playing with some other children.

Some childish sandbox crisis soon engulfed the group.
Angry words and insults, hurled like rocks,
    soon found their mark
  and brought my daughter to her knees in tears.

As I ran to intervene,
  her tormenters scattered like leaves before a wind,
    their laughter trailing behind them.

Tenderly, I pulled my daughter safe within my arms
  and held her tightly till her sobbing ceased.
While I whispered words to ease her pain,
  my thoughts knit plots of revenge
    against her enemies.
Righteous indignation boiled within my heart
  and filled my mind with angry, hateful words.

Then Your voice interrupted my thoughts, O Lord.
  I could hear You tell me to be still.

"Have you never shouted out a hurtful word
  or in anger lashed out to bring pain?"

Then I realized how well You know me, Lord,
  and how You gently teach me through my child.

You are the judge who judges with a righteous heart,
  the only one who understands our inner parts.
You see and know the fall of one small sparrow
  and hear the frightened cries of one small girl.

Help me see the places I may comfort, Lord,
  and give me strong convictions born of love.
But give me grace to count upon Your righteousness
  instead of judging others in haste.
For You have promised to avenge the helpless ones,
  and in Your time, You will set all wrongs right.

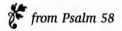 *from Psalm 58*

Facing cancer

O my God, deliver me from the enemies that surround me.
  Fear and dread, anxiety and pain dog my steps
    and fill my days and nights with restlessness.

I still cannot say the word *cancer* without a shudder,
  and I long to hold reality at a distance.
How can I face the threat of what this means
  and keep my sanity intact?

I want to watch my son run for a touchdown
  and see my daughter at her wedding,
    to bounce my grandchildren on my knee,
      to grow old with my beloved husband
        and laugh about our memories of youth.

This was not in my plans,
  and I am so afraid, Jesus.

My disease crouches at my door and mocks me,
  gloating over the power it commands.

Friends come and share their thoughts and love
  and bring their casseroles and pies.
When they go, I sink into despair again
  because I cannot bear to think of leaving them.

I long to travel, to see the world,
  to parasail, and to raft the rapids of the Colorado.
All my plans and dreams lay shattered at my feet,
  and everywhere I step, I see the shards.

Panic waits each night within my darkened room
    and prowls my days with snarling, angry growls.

O God, I wait for You but do not hear Your voice
    above the shrieking clamor of my fears.
With all my strength, I long to know Your peace,
    to climb within the fortress of Your love,
        to rest behind Your shield
           and let You fight for me,
           to feel again the pulsing of Your power.

Then will I greet the morning sun with songs again,
    despite the situations of my life.
In Your truth my fears cannot find footholds, Lord,
    and in Your arms I do not need to dread.
I praise the God who loves enough to know my pain.
    I praise the Savior who has healed my soul.
        I praise the Spirit who has filled my heart
          with hope.
I will sing once more to You, my God,
    who makes me whole.

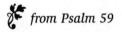 *from Psalm 59*

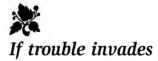

If trouble invades

You have allowed our little family
    to be blasted apart by troubles, Lord.

For so long we believed all was well,
    rejoicing in the blessings we enjoyed.
We became complacent in our satisfaction.
We forgot to focus on You
    because the here and now was so fulfilling.

Now the things we took for granted
    are a memory, and we look into the future
        with more questions than answers,
            no longer smug in our security.

We've seen our confidence broken,
    scattered in the ill wind of catastrophe.

I see my husband trying to hold on to things,
    to make a piece of all the broken parts.
He longs to make things right
        and give us hope once more,
    but even his best efforts aren't enough.

My children's eyes reflect the fear in mine,
    and I would give them faith instead of doubts,
        but I lack the answers they desire
            and feel ashamed to bare my empty hands.

Father, You have brought us to this battlefield,
    and though we sting with loss, You love us still.
Would You raise Your banner over us once more?
    Would You save and help us with Your mighty arm?

Then we will know the peace of Your deliverance
   and dwell within the tents of Your camp.
Then will we sing loud praises to our Lord and King
   and start again to build our hopes and dreams.
But this time, keep our focus on Your battle plan
   that we might know the victor's cry of joy.

from Psalm 60

When life's demands are too much

"Hear my cry, O God, listen to my prayer."

I am stretched to the limit of my endurance,
    stressed to the point of breaking.
I need to climb to a higher place,
    to see this rat race from a new perspective.

Each morning I rush to get ready for work
      and get the children off to school—
office, assignments, and deadlines never end.
In the afternoons I dash to the market, the cleaners,
      and move the children
from here to there and back again.
Then it's homework review and dinner,
    and we fall into bed with our lives all undone
      to start all over again the next day.

This isn't the place I want to be.
I want to dwell in Your quietness,
    to think and pray and meditate upon the things
      I've learned about You in Your Word.
I want my days to be counted, not cluttered,
    to be filled with quiet faith, not frantic activity.

Jesus, be the Lord of my appointment book
    and help me see the places
      I have chosen motion over meaning,
        panic over peace.
Then give me the wisdom to follow Your pace
    as I count on You to lead me day by day.

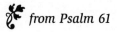 *from Psalm 61*

God's truth vs. the world's lies

I am so glad, O God, that I can rest in You.
　　You are unchangeable and everlasting.
　　　　Your promises to me will never be broken.
　　　　In You I will always be secure.

All around me people are frightened and frantic,
　　trying to build their own security
　　　　with science, philosophies, economic theories.
They wrestle with their own mortality
　　and search for ways to transcend their pain.

In You, O Lord, there is perfect peace,
　　hope that cannot be shaken,
　　　　healing that will never fail.

Help me teach my children to trust You,
　　not society's schemes.
May they reach this hurting world
　　with Your words of healing.
Keep them from being taken in by the world's lies—
　　money and status aren't true measures of worth.
If You grant them material success,
　　help them trust You, not it, for lasting peace.
I have seen the famous fall,
　　witnessed the proud and wealthy meet destruction,
　　　　seen kingdoms built on money turn to dust.
Only Your strong love lasts forever, Lord.
　　In Your time the righteous will prevail.

from Psalm 62

God's presence in a new home

O God, You are my God.
 No matter where I live, You are there.

We've moved again,
 and I am surrounded once more by the unfamiliar.
My children have no friends,
 and they are lonely and upset.
Together we sit among packing boxes and sing to You.
 As we sing, Your peace once more descends on us.

You are not a God of only one location.
 Your miracles of joy do not depend on time zones.
So we sing Your praises in a new, different place
 and find You are just the same as ever—
  offering Your love, lifting our hearts,
   fulfilling Your Word.

At night, Your stars shine overhead
 and speak Your majesty to our souls.
You draw us close within Your arms
 and tenderly shelter us in this new, unknown place.

Thank You for facing the unfamiliar with us.
 Thank You for Your truth that satisfies.
For You, O Lord, promise to uphold us
 and silence our fears with Your strong name.

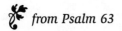 *from Psalm 63*

An unmarried daughter's pregnancy

Hear me, dear Jesus, as I cry to You
    for Your protection to surround our daughter.

She is young
    and pregnant
        and frightened,
            and, O Lord, so are we.

The baby's father wants to forget it
    like an unpleasant dream.
Our daughter's grief and shame deepen every day.

Gossip swirls around us like a rising tide
    and threatens to engulf us in its evil waves.
Self-righteous friends point with mock concern
    and cluck their tongues
        and heap their words like heavy stones
            upon our hearts.

Through it all I ache as I see my daughter's pain.
    Her sin has found her out.
        She must bear its weight.

I know this path will not be easy for us, Lord,
    but give us grace to focus on Your will for her.
Show us how to leave other people to Your care,
    and turn a deaf ear to cutting words and stares.

Although You never sinned, You know the pain it brings.
    You carried our sins for us out of Your love.
Help us show our daughter that we care for her
    enough to help her bear her burdens now.

Only You can bring a healing from this pain,
and into Your dear hands, we cast our lives.
In the end, when time completes this story, Lord,
use it to proclaim the works You have performed.

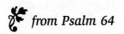 *from Psalm 64*

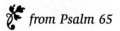

When the last child leaves home

I praise You today, my Lord and Savior,
    for I have seen the fulfillment of my vows to You.
When my children were small, I held them close
    and asked Your blessing on each one.
In full awareness of my limitations,
    I promised to teach and prepare them to follow You.

Today our youngest walks into the future
    You have prepared, excited by her prospects.
Though my eyes fill with tears,
    my heart overflows with joy
        as I reflect upon Your grace.

You fill us with so much richness, Lord—
    Your words, Spirit, presence, and forgiveness.
In crises, You are always there beside us
    with calm assurance, answering our prayers.
In our rejoicing, You rejoice with us
    and fill our home with laughter and with song.
When doubts and enemies assail us, Lord,
    You reveal a peace far greater than our fears.
You guide us each day as we rely on You,
    and every year You teach us more about Yourself.
Now we stand alone and watch our last child walk away,
    a bittersweet success that You have wrought.

I feel so rich within Your loving-kindness, Lord,
    and gratitude fills every prayer with joy.
Thank You for Your mercy that has brought us here
    and bless us with Your grace to travel on.

from Psalm 65

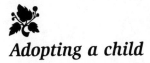

Adopting a child

I want to shout with joy,
    to sing with wild abandon:
        "The Lord is an awesome God!
            He can do the improbable, the impossible!
            No one is as great as our God!"

For years we struggled against walls of resistance,
    against policies and programs
        and bureaucrats and bullies.
But they are as nothing to You.
Before You, the sea of their paperwork parted,
    and we walked through today
        on the dry ground of victory!

Today we hold our adopted son in our arms.
    Yesterday I did not know this precious little boy;
        today I am his mother!

So many times I raised my prayers to You
    and often wept with despair at my heart's longing.
I recall the hours spent watching other women,
        longing to be a mother too,
    to know the softness of a baby's cheek on my neck,
        to feel tiny fingers brush my lips.

Days, months, years of longing have turned to memory.
In my arms Your answer to our prayers smiles up at me.
How can I offer You enough to show my gratitude?
    What can I sacrifice to show my love?

Then in my arms the answer sighs and waves his hands
    as if he heard the questions of my heart.
Yes, Jesus, I will offer back my son to You.

Each day I'll sing Your praises in his ears.
I'll teach his little feet to walk along Your paths
   and focus his bright eyes upon Your Word.

Praise be to God,
   who hears and answers all our prayers
      and does not keep Himself outside our pain.

Praise be to Him
   who sees the lonely, breaking heart
      and heals it with His everlasting love.

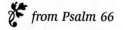 *from Psalm 66*

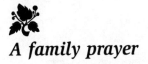

A family prayer

In our little family circle,
    we join our hands and bow our heads in prayer.

May God's gracious blessings always fill our home.
    Whenever we look into each other's eyes,
        may we see the love of Jesus shining there.

As we work and play,
    may others see Your justice, Lord,
        in all we do and say.

Remind us that all we have—
    all we are or ever will be—
        is a gift from Your right hand.

We praise You, God,
    for You are mighty and merciful,
        strong and tender,
            ever guiding us with Your love.

Teach us to do Your will in all our ways
    so that Your earthly harvest might be bountiful.

We thank You, God, for this and every day,
    a precious gift of time You have prepared for us.

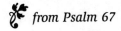 *from Psalm 67*

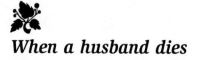

When a husband dies

Arise, O God, and scatter the enemies of my peace.
    Blow away the fear and doubt and loneliness,
        like smoke before the wind.
Melt the aching of my heart with Your love,
    like wax melts in the sunlight.

I long to feel joy again,
    to have a thought that is not edged in sadness,
        to sleep and dream and wake
            without tear-filled eyes.

It has been months since my beloved husband died,
    and still the pain is fresh and sharp.
My children play and go to school,
    eat and sleep and face the routine of each day,
        but their daddy's absence colors every hour.
There is an emptiness in our hearts, dear Jesus.
    An unrelenting shadow stalks our every step.

You have promised to be a father to the fatherless,
    to defend the widow in her solitary plight,
        to set the lonely in families
            and bring us again to a place of singing.

We need to hear Your song again,
    to feel our souls drenched
        with the cool refreshing rain
            of Your contentment.

I am dwelling in a valley of sorrow,
    and I long to climb the mountain of Your strength.
I need to see from a high place once more,
    to regain my perspective, to look ahead, not back.

I want to give my children joy again,
    to laugh and shout and run
        and fling my arms in wild abandon.
But I am choked and dry,
    parched within the desert of my grief.

Flood me with the water that can give me life again.
    Fill me up and splash it over till my children see
        that life goes on with God.

I long to show them You are enough
    to fill the emptiness now and always.
They need to know You love them
    with a love stronger than their pain.
But I cannot show them that without Your power, Lord,
    for I am filled with nothing on my own.

Grant me courage to carry on,
    to walk each day, confident in Your assurance
        that I do not walk alone.
Turn our faces to the glory of Your future
    and give us grace to walk away
        from our fear and insecurity.

We claim Your mighty power to enable us,
    Your strength to raise our voices now in praise.
We place our trembling hands
        in Your great ones, dear Lord,
    and beg You to hold us as we journey on.

from Psalm 68

When overwhelmed by activity

Save me, O God,
    for I think I am in over my head!
I am sinking in the sea of my commitments,
    engulfed by needs greater than my time or energy.
I keep looking for You amid my cluttered life,
    but I cannot see Your face over the obstacles.

Each job I accepted,
    each responsibility I accrued,
        seemed small at the time—just one more thing.
Now I find my days and nights
    crowded with appointments, meetings, briefings—
        one more after one more after one more.

I never seem to have a moment
    to listen to my children,
        to talk with my husband,
            to meditate on Your Word.
My house reflects my neglect,
    and my family thinks home-cooked meals
        come in cans and boxes
            and you just add water.
People in my church and neighborhood
    see me coming and going,
        but I'm never still long enough to talk.

I need Your guidance, Lord.
    Please rescue me from my inability to say no.
Set my feet upon a strong rock of resolve
    and keep me from drowning in this sea I've made.
Reorder my priorities according to Your direction.

Still my fear of those I might disappoint
    when I resign or quit or refuse to take the job.

I see so clearly that I sought
    peace and acceptance from others
        and ignored the contentment You give in Christ.
I have sacrificed the harmony of my home
    to the cacophony of my over-burdened schedule.
I do not want to continue
    this overwhelming tide of activity.
I long to sit once more at Your feet,
    to hear Your still, small voice,
        to have time to reflect and answer.

Remind me of what I know to be true, Lord—
    You desire praise more than frenzied activity;
        quiet thanksgiving more than noisy sacrifice;
          obedience to You rather than to others.
Forgive my self-centered ambition
    and set me once more on Your path.
Help me rebuild the trust of my family
        so we may rest in our eternal inheritance
    and dwell together in the harmony of Your grace.

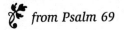 *from Psalm 69*

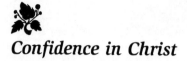

Confidence in Christ

There is so much fear in the world, Jesus.
 Today I talked with a mother who is terrified—
  of violence and disease, of technology,
   of politics, and of society in general.
She is anxious about things she cannot see
 and does not understand.
Unwittingly, she transfers her fear to her children.
I see it in their eyes
 and hear it in their voices.
They lack hope and a vision
 because their mother's fears have blinded them.

Help me transmit to my children
 a different view of life.
Help me show them the pitfalls of the world
 balanced with the knowledge
  of the joyful life You give.
Let my words and actions portray
 the confidence I have through Your salvation.
Make my family a light in the darkness,
 a source of hope for the hopeless,
  helpful to those in need,
   and encouraging to those who are afraid.

For You are greater than the world, O God,
 and are exalted evermore!
You are never overcome by evil
 but overcame evil with Your goodness.
You, O Jesus, are the one who helps and delivers
 all who call on Your powerful name.

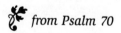 *from Psalm 70*

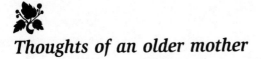

Thoughts of an older mother

In You, O Lord, I have always taken refuge.
Keep me from being "put out to pasture"
    by my children and grandchildren.

For so long I was the one
        to whom they went for help and advice.
            They sought comfort from me.
Now as they listen to me, I see something other
        than respect or attentiveness in their eyes.
They ask my opinion because it is expected—
            the kind thing to do,
        a way to make me feel part of their lives.

From my earliest days, I trusted You, dear Jesus.
I raised my family and taught my children
        from Your holy Scriptures.
Together we prayed and sang Your praises
        and memorized Your beautiful words of promise.

Now, I feel as if my children have left me behind,
        like a relic of their past—
            irrelevant and unnecessary.
I thought the challenges of raising children
            would be my greatest,
        but, Lord, these days are trying
            in new and unexpected ways.

Do not cast me away now that I am old.
        Do not forsake me because my strength is gone.
Stay close to me, my precious Lord,
        for I need You more than ever.
I cannot move as quickly as I used to,
        my energy lags behind my good intentions,

and the days end with unfinished tasks.
I do not want to be a complaining old woman
    or drive away my family
        with whines and nagging needs.

Will You help me now as You have always done?
    Grant me grace not to feel sorry for myself.
Let me still tell others of Your righteousness
    and sing of Your mercy and love.
You have taught me since my youth,
    and I will never stop declaring
        Your marvelous deeds.
Even though I am old now, and my hair is silver,
        even though my step is not as springy
            as in my youth,
    You, my Lord, have not changed.
I will tell my grandchildren and great-grandchildren
    of Your power and grace,
        for You have done great things for me.
Comfort me now as You have in the past
    for You are my Redeemer and friend.

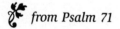 *from Psalm 71*

Prayer for children's continued growth

I watch my children as they sleep
    and pray Your blessings on them, Lord.
Let them grow strong in body and mind.
Guide them as they follow You in their youth
        and give them courage
    to walk in Your counsel day by day.
May they make wise decisions
    according to Your Word and will.
Grant them kind hearts and gentle spirits
    to see and understand the hurts of others.
But give them strength of character as well,
    so they may stand for righteousness and truth.
Give them pleasant days to learn to laugh and play
        mixed with days of difficulty that teach them
            to lean on You for the strength they lack.

As they grow, mold me into the mother
    You would have me be.
Help me lead by example, not in words alone.
Give me grace to ask for forgiveness when I'm wrong
    and grace to grant it when they slip and fall.
Keep me from expecting my children
        to fulfill my dreams.
Grant me wisdom to know when to stand firm
    and when to move aside.

You alone can lead me with a steady hand.
    You alone can love these children more than I.
Keep me close beside You as I train them
        that they might honor You in all they do and say.

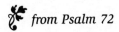 *from Psalm 72*

Why do unbelievers prosper?

Lord, I know of Your goodness to Your children
    and have memorized Your promises.
I have studied and even taught others Your words.
Yet there are times when doubts creep into my mind.

I look at our family and other believers
    and wonder at the pain and trials
        endured by Your children.
All around us people mock Your name,
    using it as an expletive.
They revel in their independence from God
    and taunt those who call upon You.
When my children mention Jesus at school,
    or include a reference to the Bible in a report,
        they are reprimanded.
But those who flaunt their disbelief in You
    are praised as independent thinkers,
        unfettered by archaic and mythic beliefs.
The godless prosper in business
    and freely argue their points of view
        on television and in papers and magazines.

My children ask why You allow
        the evil in the world to grow
    and let those who love You suffer condemnation.
When I try to explain it, I become confused also.
    So I meditate on Your Word
        and seek You in the quiet of Your sanctuary.
There, You open my mind
    and give me eyes to view eternity.
You are so great and gracious to me, Lord,
    giving insight when I'm blinded
        by my earthly bent.

This life is just a stop on the way to eternity.
The foundations we build here
    will face the tide of Your final evaluation.
Those built upon the rock of Jesus Christ will stand
    and hear Your call to enter.
But those who build on the slippery ground
        of their own making
    will see their earthly kingdoms swept away,
        as dreams vanish in the brightening dawn.

Forgive me for my envy of others' earthly success,
    for failing to recall Your plans for us.
Help me teach my children to look beyond
        the here and now
    and focus on their rich inheritance from You.

Thank You for holding us firmly in Your strong hand;
    for providing counsel when we cannot see the way;
        for showing us that although we slip and fall,
            You are our strength and will lead us on.

 *from Psalm 73*

If a natural disaster strikes

Are You angry with us, Lord?
Is that why You allowed this natural disaster
    to destroy what we have built?
As we pick our way through the home we loved,
    gathering shredded mementos from the rubble,
        we wonder if You really care about us.

We prayed for a miracle as we saw the terror near
    and raised our voices, calling for Your mercy.
But no miracle came;
    no hand held back the onslaught.
We watched the devastation run unchecked,
    leaving in its wake our dreams,
        a memory on the wind.
Now the sun mocks us with its gentle warmth
    as teasing breezes brush our cheeks and hair.

My children stand silently beside me,
    overwhelmed with feelings they cannot express.
In my confusion, I long to ease their pain,
    but answers do not come.
        I am confused as well.
Aren't You the God who split the seas apart,
    who fed thousands from the desert's void?
Your fingers formed the sun and moon and stars
    and set the boundaries of the land and sea.

In this silence, I strain to hear Your voice,
    to know what word of truth to tell my children.
Lacking peace, I bow my head and heart before You.
    Lord, have mercy on my faintly flickering faith.

Day and night You made,
    and the seasons in their endless march
      follow the plan that You set.
Flood and fire and wind and all the elements
    are subject to Your majesty alone.

Forgive me for the selfishness this loss brings,
    for looking to the here and now, not to You.
In Your mercy, You have always cared for me
    with tender kindness from Your heart of love.

Set my face once more toward Yours.
    Give me courage to carry on.
Strengthen my trust in You
    and help me place my family in Your care
    as I offer encouragement to those around me.
For You are truly God, our great defender,
    and this trial is no disaster in Your hands.
We will rebuild and find voices once more
    to sing to You and praise Your holy name.

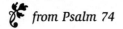 *from Psalm 74*

When tempted to manipulate a child's life

I give thanks to You, O God.
    I give thanks and raise Your name on high
        and tell others of Your wonderful acts.

You know the right time for all things—
    the time for births and deaths,
        for great joys and deepest sorrows.

It is You who lifts one up to power
    and brings another down in defeat.

Dear Jesus, keep me from meddling in Your work,
    maneuvering this child or that one
        into a position of advantage;
        pushing, prodding, promulgating plans
            that I have manufactured to get ahead.

Instead, show me how to be satisfied with obedience
    and choose the path that follows You.
Teach me to guide my children's trust in You
    and place their futures in Your hands as well.

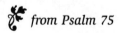 *from Psalm 75*

Prayer for the nation

In our land, O God, You were once known
    and Your name was announced among the people!
In private and public, we were not ashamed
    to give You honor and to praise Your deeds.

In wars our sons and daughters fought and died
    and prayed their prayers
        and sang their hymns aloud.

Now Your name is mocked and faith denied
    by old and young who seek other gods.
Those who cry for freedom from all creeds
    search for meaning in the void they've made.

Help those of us in families of faith
    cease our silence and proclaim Your truth,
        teach our children of their heritage,
            and show our neighbors the hope to live by.

Keep us from the maelstrom of despair
        that threatens to undo the land we love.
Give us hearts to keep our vows to You
    that rulers may once more govern with truth.

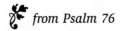 *from Psalm 76*

When fears deny sleep

At night I lie upon my bed, O Lord,
 seeking, but not finding, rest.
I recite Scriptures, pray my prayers,
 but still sleep eludes me.
Instead, I think of my children—
 growing, changing, maturing,
  leaving behind the security of childhood.

My mind scurries
 from one fear to another,
  like a frantic mouse seeking escape.

Dramatic and terrifying scenarios loom before me
 fed by newspapers, magazines, and television.
I envision my children kidnaped, brainwashed,
 twisted in mind and body by some unnamed villain.
In my waking dreams, I am impotent to help,
 paralyzed with doubt and fear.

In the daylight, I can push away the darker thoughts,
 but in the quiet stillness of the night,
  they tiptoe back to haunt me.

Then into the mist of my fearful fancies,
 a bold idea shines its light:
 I will recall the deeds You have performed, O Lord,
  and meditate on Your mighty works.
From the beginning of time, You have protected Your own,
 performing miracles to rescue Your children.
Nature listens and obeys Your commands,
 and nations rise and fall within Your plans.

Even in the universe of our family,
    we have seen Your blessings time and time again.
Your grace and mercy led us through the storms of life,
    and You promise never to forsake us.

Although I cannot see Your face or trace Your footprints,
    I recognize the imprint of Your love, Jesus.
Why should I choose to cling to my dark fears
    when You have given me access to Your light?
I will lie down and trust the future to Your care
    and rest myself within Your gentle arms.

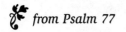 *from Psalm 77*

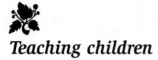

Teaching children

What a privilege You have given me, Lord—
    to be a mother to these little ones
        and to teach and guide them each day.

I look at their eager faces filled with wonder,
    their minds bubbling over with questions,
        and I am awed with the enormity of the task.
How can I share with them knowledge of You, O God,
    so they will not merely parrot my beliefs
        but forge a deep, lasting personal faith?
What can I say to frame Your works and words
    in terms they understand?

Use me, Lord Jesus, to reflect Your love
    to my children.
Give me creative ideas to share Your Word
    so they will comprehend its meaning and truth.
Keep me close beside You so I will hear
    Your still, small voice before I speak.
Set a guard upon my mouth
    so all I say reflects Your gentleness.
And Lord, if You desire to call my children
    to Your service, give me strength to let them go,
        knowing that You have beckoned them.

I thank You for the trust You've placed in me
    by giving little lives into my care.
I pledge my efforts and my energies
    to raise up sons and daughters
        who know and love Your name.

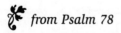 *from Psalm 78*

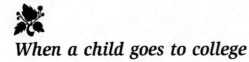

When a child goes to college

O God, those who dwell in the halls of higher learning
　　have invaded Your inheritance.
　　　　They have insulted You before our children
　　　　　　and have attacked the foundations of faith.

In front of their fellow students,
　　our children have been ridiculed and torn apart
　　　　for holding to the tenets of Your Word.
They have been held up as objects of reproach,
　　scorned as nonthinkers,
　　　　derided as naive and unenlightened
　　　　　　before their peers.

As a mother, my heart aches to see my children mocked,
　　yet I know that through this crucible,
　　　　You can perfect a pure and solid faith,
　　　　　　one unable to be shaken
　　　　　　　　by mere human philosophy.

I can no longer protect and shield them
　　from the anger the world hurls at You
　　　　and those who love Your name.
Give them strength of character
　　and passion to cling to their commitment
　　　　despite the antagonism of atheism.

Keep them steadfast on the straight path of truth,
　　no matter how beguiling
　　　　the crooked path of deceit appears.

Enlighten their minds with Your Spirit's wisdom
　　when they are tempted to believe
　　　　the enemy's clever lies.

I have sent my children into the battle, Jesus,
     and though I know they face tremendous foes,
  I trust Your power
     to bring them through victorious.

You are the one they have believed in
     from their earliest days,
  and You will not forsake them
     now that they are grown.

How good it is to know that You are
     in the college classroom with them,
        guiding and directing every hour.
I sing Your praises once again, my Savior,
     for You have never failed to keep Your own.

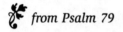 *from Psalm 79*

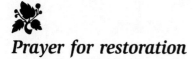

Prayer for restoration

O Father, hear my cry to You.
    I have not been diligent
        in leading my children in Your ways.

I began with such good intentions,
    reading Bible stories, saying daily prayers,
        talking about You with my little ones,
            singing songs to You with them.

Then my days were filled with other things.
    Neighbors and committees and classes,
        housework and school work and busy work
            crowded out the time to sing and pray.

At first I hardly noticed how our habits changed.
Then little things crept in
    to steal our minds and hearts
        a few moments at a time.

Hours and days and weeks
    are now filled with meaningless activity,
        and I feel my soul and spirit
            shrinking bit by bit.

Forgive me, Lord, and restore my joy in You.
    Shower me again with the warmth of Your approval.
Plant within my heart the seed of faith
    and bless it so it will grow strong in You.
Nurture me like a choice vine within Your garden.
    Water me with Your Word and with Your love.
Sink my roots deep into Your grace
    that I may be Your witness to my children.

Revive me as a mother, Lord,
and I will strive to never turn away again.
Only in Your presence is there true joy
and only in following Your path can I find peace.

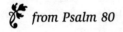 *from Psalm 80*

Joy on a Sunday morning

Thank You, God, for Sundays
    when we go to church together as a family.
Sitting in the pews,
        children stair-stepped at our side,
            my heart swells with praise to You.

Sharing the hymnal with my husband
        and hearing his deep-voiced harmony
            fills me with a rare contentment.
This time in Your house is truly peace-full.

Braids and ponytails,
        crew cuts standing at attention,
            nodding in time to the organ's interlude.
When the offering basket passes by,
        I smile to see a dirty quarter reverently added.

They are learning, growing, changing
        day by day to be the people You have intended.
How I love to witness each small step along the way.

Here in Your house, You feed us
        with Your Word and Sacrament.
As we leave, You fill us with Your blessing,
        then gently lead us from our Sunday worship
            to walk each day sustained by faith and grace.

We trust ourselves to Your loving care
        and seek to live our lives according to Your will.

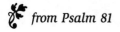 *from Psalm 81*

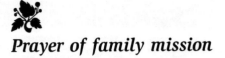

Prayer of family mission

O Lord, as we join our hands
    again around this table,
        we thank You for the abundance we enjoy.

But we are mindful, too,
    of those who suffer in our world.

We pray Your strength for those who have no champion.
    We ask Your care for those who need a father's love.

For those who struggle against oppressors, Lord,
    we ask Your intercession and Your peace.

Let us not be so complacent in our plenty
    that we forget the needy and hurting at our door.

Give us the eyes and ears of Jesus
    to see and hear their plight.
    Make us His hands and feet to offer help.

We know You will come to judge the nations
    in Your time.
Keep us busy with Your work till then.

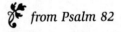 *from Psalm 82*

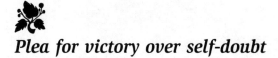

Plea for victory over self-doubt

O God, let me hear Your voice.
    Give me an inner ear attuned to Your direction.

Sometimes the clamor of motherhood
    drowns out the stillness of Your peace,
        and my old enemies rally around,
            claiming my attention once again.

Worry and self-doubt attack first,
    hurling darts of fear to wound my resolve.
Then fretfulness, impatience, and anger join the fight,
    defeating me with hopelessness and guilt.

I know You have the power to vanquish these enemies
    for I have seen Your victories before.

Chase away these thoughts and patterns of defeat
    so I may be the mother You desire.
Burn them from my mind with Your consuming love
    and render them powerless by Your forgiving touch.

Let me follow You, my Captain, as an obedient soldier
        on the battlefields I face each day
    that I might taste the victory You offer
        to those who pledge allegiance to Your name.

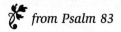 *from Psalm 83*

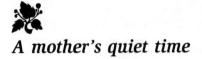

A mother's quiet time

How lovely it is in Your presence, Lord.
    When the children are at school or napping,
        I enter my room, close the door,
            and kneel to quietly speak with You.

My soul is so hungry for this time each day—
    the moments when You and I converse.
        It is as if I find a refuge here—
            a place of rest and refreshment.

I praise You, God, for You are truly mighty.
    Your sovereign wisdom never fails.
        Your strength is great; mighty is Your power.
            Yet You stoop to touch a mother's heart.

I come once more, confessing that I need You,
    especially when I have tried to take control.
        Forgive my selfish will that seeks its own way
            and grant me grace to wait upon You, Lord.

I bring my children to You one by one, Jesus,
    and ask You to guide and bless them today.
        Help them see You as their source of strength
            when temptations and worries block their way.
They seem so small and vulnerable to me,
    but I know with You they can face the fiercest foe
        and be victorious because You stand beside them.
Direct each step they take
    until they stand before Your throne,
        robed in the majesty of Your grace—
            forgiven, restored, renewed for all eternity.

I ask these things on behalf of my children
 because I know You never withhold goodness
  from those who walk with You.
You have promised to bless those who trust You
 so I boldly bring my petitions to Your throne.

How lovely it is to have this time of prayer, Lord,
 when the children are at school or napping,
  and I enter my room, close the door,
   and kneel humbly in Your presence again.

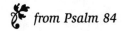 *from Psalm 84*

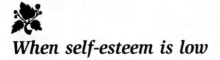

When self-esteem is low

You have shown me Your favor, Lord,
    and rescued me from a past
        that threatened to destroy me.
When I was without hope,
    You forgave me and restored my sense of worth.
You covered my sin with Your perfection
    and blotted out my transgressions with Your love.

But I look at my children and my old fears return.
    Can I be the mother they need
        despite the experiences of my past?
Am I too damaged to raise them
    free from the influence of my old ways?

Then Your calming words return once more to me:
    "I am the God who rejoices in restoration.
    I promise peace to My people and keep them
        from returning to past mistakes.
    My salvation is near to all who fear Me.
    And My glory resides within my children forever.
    My love and faithfulness embrace you.
    My peace and righteousness fall on you
        like summer rains.
    I will give you only what is good,
        and you will see the harvest in your children.
    I will go before you every day
        and prepare the way for every step you take."

from Psalm 85

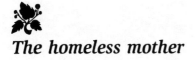

The homeless mother

"Hear, O LORD, and answer me,
for I am poor and needy."

Guard my life from those around me,
for I have put my trust in You.
Those around me look at me with scorn
or turn their backs and quickly walk away.

I am a mother of the streets,
living on the edge of a society
that wishes I would disappear
so it could be free of me and my needs.

But I remember, Jesus,
when You walked the land so long ago.
You saw and touched mothers living there
and lifted up their children and embraced them.
I'm sure You'd do the same for me today,
if You were walking this city street.
For You are a God who doesn't judge me
like the world does
or value me because of what I own or wear.
You have looked beyond my eyes into my heart,
and there You touched my soul and gave it life.

Though others may despise or disregard me, Lord,
I know Your face will always turn my way.
In Your mercy, You have granted strength to me
to face the challenge of each day.

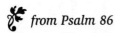 *from Psalm 86*

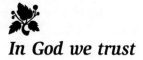

In God we trust

Long ago we were a country
   that loved You, Lord,
      and You made Your face to shine upon us.

Families came from distant lands
   to savor freedom and blessings from Your hand.

And You were faithful to Your Word
   and prospered those who called upon Your name.

But now our children are taught
   their success comes from their own ingenuity;
      their prosperity is a product of their pride.

Use us as parents to turn our children's hearts to You.
Show us how to teach them
   of Your mercy, grace, and goodness.

Forgive our prideful boasting, Lord,
      and give us humble spirits
   that seek to lead our country along a righteous path
      so we may know Your blessings again.

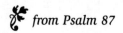 *from Psalm 87*

Overcoming post-partum depression

"O LORD, the God who saves me,
　　day and night I cry out before You."
Hear my prayer as I raise it to Your throne;
　　listen and help me, for I cannot help myself.

As I look around, I know I should rejoice.
　　I have a new baby,
　　　　a lovely home,
　　　　　　a husband who loves me,
　　　　　　　　and friends who care.
Though my eyes see these things,
　　my heart is blind to them.
　　　　My soul is weighted with dark despair.
I cannot smile or sing
　　or even raise my voice in prayer,
　　　　except to cry out in pain to You, dear Jesus.
Am I going crazy?
　　Tears fill my eyes and overflow unbidden.
　　　　Dark thoughts of self-destruction fill my mind.
　　　　　　I feel my grip on reality slipping bit by bit.

I am filled with fears:
　　that I cannot be a good mother,
　　that the future is too overwhelming,
　　that this tiny child needs more than I can give.

My only escape is to hide
　　from all that seems to threaten me.
I feel myself retreating into the darkness—
　　a darkness whose pull I feel powerless to escape.

It is like a relentless current,
 surrounding and engulfing me—
  a seductive friend,
   smothering me with terror.

I raise my hands to You in anguished supplication.
 Hear me, Jesus, and take my hand in Yours.
  Pull me from the pit of this depression.
   Set me on the rock of faith once more.
You are the only one who understands me.
 Please help me out of my own helplessness.

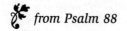 *from Psalm 88*

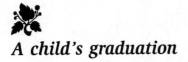

A child's graduation

I will sing of Your great love forever
 and tell others of Your unending faithfulness.
You, O Lord, have protected and directed this child
 of ours for 18 years.
Now he stands before us in cap and gown.

My mother's heart swells with laughter and tears
 as I hold my husband's hand and watch our son.

Your hand has been upon his life since he was born—
 protecting, leading, loving, disciplining.

I recall Your help with the struggles of life's stages:
 teaching him to walk, to talk,
  to tie his shoes, to say his prayers.
Was it so long ago he struggled with spelling
 or pondered the mysteries of multiplication?
The days of childhood seemed long and endless,
 yet now they're past—the child becomes a man.

I know You have created the universe,
 the earth, the mountains, and the seas,
  yet here before me stands miracle enough.
As You have brought him this far, Lord,
 would You now lead him on?
You have begun a good work in his heart,
 would You complete it as he walks
  along the path You have set before him?
Guide his choices that he may always heed Your Word,
 follow Your Son,
  and listen intently to Your Spirit's direction.

I gave him to You when I first held him in my arms,
and I renew that vow today.

Guard and guide my son, O God.
Show him how to face his future
with both courage and humility;
Grant him the courage to seek Your will
and the humility to obey it.

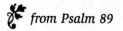 *from Psalm 89*

Prayer for wisdom and faithfulness

Lord, You have been my dwelling place
    for as long as I can recall.
I have experienced the faith of past generations
    and have enjoyed the fruit of their prayers.

But even before the first person walked the earth,
    You were there, preparing in love
        for Your creation.
You are not limited by time or space
    or any other created thing.
I stand amazed at the wonder of Your grace
    in revealing Yourself to me—
        a woman, wife, mother.
Who am I that You should lavish such abundance on me?

In Your sovereign power,
    You know all my secret sins.
        You see my weak attempts at goodness,
            my bungled job of being Your disciple.
In the big scheme of things,
    who am I but a tiny blip
        on the timeline of eternity?
I may live and work for 70 or 80 years
    and pass from this world into the next,
        and what then, O Lord and Savior?

Teach me to value each day,
    every relationship, each conversation
        as an opportunity from You to share Your love.
Enlighten me with Your creativity
    when I am puzzled and confused
        about situations within my family.

Grant me Your insights and wisdom
    as I guide these children You have given us.
Keep me from the temptations to lose my temper,
    to say the first thing in my mind,
        to judge without listening,
            to discipline without love.

In Your compassion,
    satisfy me with Your unfailing love each day
        that I may be strengthened
            for the tasks You've given.
Fill my heart with gladness so it will overflow
    in thanksgiving and praise to You.
May my children see in me
    a reflection of Your love
        as they walk with You as Your own.
Establish my work of mothering
    so that my labors will not be in vain
        and in future generations,
            these small seeds will bear much fruit.

from Psalm 90

Reflections on God's goodness

I gather my frightened child onto my lap,
 and in the quiet of the night,
  we rock together in the old oak chair.

Moonlight streams through the window,
 making patterns on the bedroom wall,
  and the little one within my arms
   burrows deep in my embrace.

"Do not fear my child,
 for God is with you and will comfort you.
He will enfold you with His love
 like a hen covers her chicks
  with warm and downy feathers.
He will always be faithful to you
 and will stand beside you,
  no matter what the day or evening brings.
You may see many frightening things,
 but God will always be near you,
  offering His protection and His power.
Because your heart is in His keeping,
 nothing will be able to take you from His care.
He will send His angels
 to stand guard over you,
  protecting you from harm,
   directing you into paths of safety.
No matter what happens,
 you can always call on the name of Jesus,
  and He will hear and answer you,
   not because you are always good
    but because He is always great."

Slowly, almost imperceptibly, I feel my child relax
    and recognize the gentle rhythm of her calming heart.
I, too, sigh in peace and wonder,
    amazed once more at Your unfailing love.

🌿 *from Psalm 91*

When a mother embarrasses a child

It is good to praise You, O Lord,
    and make music to Your name, O Most High,
        to proclaim Your love in the morning
            and Your faithfulness at night!

Unless, of course, you are the mother of teenagers!

I was singing at the top of my voice the other day
    when my son trooped in with several friends.
How was I to know they would be arriving
    in the midst of my private concert?
Later, he told me it was embarrassing to have a mother
    who fancied herself a religious songbird.
I replied it was uncontrollable joy
    pouring from my heart.
He suggested I could perhaps control my joy,
    at least when his friends were around.
I answered that joy was a funny thing—
    you just never knew when it was going to pop out!
He gave me his best "Oh, Mom" look
    and shook his head in resignation.
I grabbed him for a quick hug
    before he could escape into his room.

You have given me such blessings, Father.
    My heart overflows with praises to You.
Thank You for the song You have placed in my soul—
    don't ever let me be afraid or embarrassed
        to belt it out!

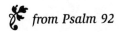 *from Psalm 92*

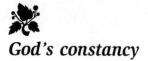

God's constancy

You reign, O Lord, robed in majesty
    and armed with strength.
You have created the world
    and all those in it,
        and Your laws are established for eternity.

I am so grateful for Your unchanging nature
    in the midst of a society
        that teaches my children
            "nothing lasts forever."

You provide a message of hope and truth
    that will carry my sons and daughters
        throughout their lives.

You are mightier than human whims.
    Your laws and principles stand firm.
        Your ways are righteous and holy.
            You can be depended upon forever.

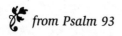 *from Psalm 93*

If a husband loses his job

O Lord, the God who avenges,
    shine forth and let me leave my hurt with You.
Keep me from seeking retribution,
    from lashing out at those who show no mercy
        and rejoice in the downfall of the weak.

Accusations have brought down my husband's career.
    A lifetime of work and dreams lies in shambles.

There are those who rejoice in his downfall,
    arrogantly boasting of their own integrity,
        lauding the purity of their motives and lifestyle
          while sneering with contempt
            at their fallen comrade.

Their remarks wound me
    and shake the faith of our children
        as surely as a bullet or knife
          would pierce our hearts.

They shake their heads with righteous indignation
    and question the validity of our faith in You.
You know the things they cannot see, Father.
    You understand the secrets we hide from ourselves.

I know Your discipline can bring blessing from pain
    and healing that transcends the hurt we feel.

Will You give me grace to count on You,
    to deal with all the anger I now feel?
I need Your help to keep from slipping in the dark—
    Your hand to steady me so I won't fall.

Let me be an example to my family,
　　leading them within the fortress of Your strength.
As this battle rages around us,
　　help us find refuge in the rock that never moves.
Let us cling to Your strong name.
　　In You alone we find security and salvation.

from Psalm 94

Praise to God for His faithfulness

With joy I sing to You, O Lord,
    and come into Your presence with thanksgiving.
Music wells within my heart,
    and I raise my voice to You.

Your greatness is greater than all the wonders
        in the world,
    and in Your majesty, our family is secure.

There is no pain so deep that Your hand
    cannot reach us and bring us out.
Nor are there problems so towering
    that You cannot lift us beyond them.

Oceans obey You,
    and the dry land calls You Master.

You made each of us,
    and You are the one before whom we bow.

Keep our little flock safe, dearest Shepherd Jesus.
Guide us daily so we won't stray,
    becoming lost and afraid.

Keep my heart pliable in Your hand
    so I may be the mother my children need—
        the mother You desire me to be.

Lead me into the restful, sweet assurance—
    the peacefulness of heart You lavish
        on all Your children.

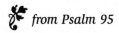 *from Psalm 95*

When a child enters God's service

I sing a new song to You, O Lord,
  for You have called my child
    to proclaim Your salvation.
He has determined to declare Your glory
    among the nations,
  to tell of Your marvelous deeds
    among the peoples of the world.

From birth I dedicated this child to You,
  lifting him before You in prayer.
I told him of Your loving-kindness,
    Your wisdom and mercy;
  pointed his eyes heavenward
    to see Your majestic and splendid universe;
      directed his feet to walk the earth
        dependent on Your strength and grace.

But a mother can only walk so far with her child,
    can only lead him to the brink
      of his own life with You.
Then the child walks alone,
    subject to his own will—not his mother's.

What joy to see his choices guided by You,
    to see the fruit of tiny seeds
      planted years earlier.
Your faithfulness, not mine,
    brought forth the harvest, Lord,
  yet You have allowed me to share the celebration.

I offer thanks and worship Your name
    and stand before Your throne in prayerful awe.
For You have called my child into Your service
    and given him the task
        of sharing Your kingdom with others.

Let jubilation fill our hearts with songs of praise.
    Let joy sound forth from everyone who hears.

The Lord is faithful.
    He hears and answers mothers' prayers
        and sends His blessings
            to our children's children.

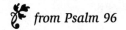 *from Psalm 96*

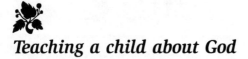

Teaching a child about God

Lord, help me find a balance
    as I teach my children about You.
I have a tendency to speak only
       of Your grace and mercy,
    the comfort of forgiveness and peace.
I love to point to gentle Jesus in the manger
    or describe His soothing touch that healed.
But do I ignore the righteous anger You displayed,
    Your fiery judgment reserved for sin?

In the majestic mystery of Your power,
    fierce light that purges evil
       as sunlight melts wax,
    Your righteous, shining glory cannot be denied.

Give me wisdom to hold before my child
    the truth of Your greatness,
       not just comforting platitudes.
Let me accurately describe
       how love and fear, mercy and judgment
          all find fulfillment in Your name,
    how purity demands perfection
       yet offers forgiveness,
    how evil is destroyed while peace prevails.

Through the prompting of Your Holy Spirit, Lord,
    give me the words and actions that I need
       to help my children love with holy awe
          the God who loved them first
             and now resides within their hearts.

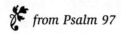 *from Psalm 97*

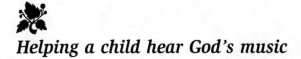

Helping a child hear God's music

Lord, give me a new song to sing with my children,
    a song that tells of Your marvelous deeds,
        not only in the time of Abraham or Daniel
            or Jesus or Paul but today—here and now.

Help me teach my children to look with fresh eyes
    at the world they face,
        discovering Your faithfulness day by day.
May they compose their own songs, shouts of joy,
    music that is suitable to singing Your praises
        in this time and place.

Give us ears to hear Your voice
    resonating in the world around us—
        crashing in the waves,
            singing in the wind,
                laughing in the river rapids.

Help me, O Lord, to tune my children's ears
        to hear Your voice in all things
    and to join in with their unique songs of praise.
For You created music as a gift for our hearts—
    a way to share Your message with the world.

Swell our hearts with chords and melodies of love
    that we might fill the earth
        with songs of heavenly peace.

from Psalm 98

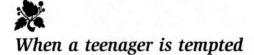

When a teenager is tempted

The world raises high its idols
    before my children, Lord—
        MONEY   BEAUTY   FAME
    all glisten enticingly from their golden pedestals.

Yet You are King, reigning in holiness.

"Come follow us," false gods call.
    "We'll bring you happiness, friends, popularity."

Yet You are King, reigning in holiness.

"Don't listen to the old ways!" they whisper.
    "Be free to feel and do and know all things!"

Yet You are King, reigning in holiness.

Little do my children know,
    drunk with the wine of adolescence,
        that there is a freedom that leads to slavery,
        a beauty that turns to ugliness,
            a popularity that breeds contempt
                and bitter loneliness.

They do not wish to see You
    as their King, reigning in holiness.

Bring them through this time as You did
    Your chosen people of old,
    speaking to their hearts through cloud and fire,
        leading with justice tempered with forgiveness,
            guiding them to the land You have prepared.

One day may they stand in awe-filled wonder,
    worshiping their God with hands outstretched.
Then will they sing a song of great adoration:
    "O God, You are our King who reigns forever."

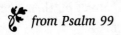 *from Psalm 99*

Prayer to teach by example

Jesus, let my service always be
    offered with gladness and joy.
May my children see in my behavior
    my belief that You are indeed my Lord and Savior.

Give me courage to teach them they aren't on their own,
    cast adrift on the world's shifting seas
        to find their way as best they can.

Direct them, instead, to this great truth:
    They are each one Yours—
        created, bought, and paid for
            with Your precious blood.

Guide them to enter Your gates
    as obedient sheep
filled with praise and thanksgiving
    for You, their loving Shepherd.

For Your goodness and love endure forever.
    Your faithfulness continues
        through all generations.

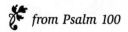 *from Psalm 100*

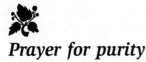

Prayer for purity

As a mother I often teach and preach,
    give directions and corrections.
Yet You have spoken to me, Lord,
    about keeping my own "heart house" clean.
You have convicted me of my need for repentance,
    for holy living before I try to show others Your ways.

Give me eyes to see the dark and dusty corners
    that need cleansing, Lord—
        places I have stored my private sins,
            safely tucked away,
                not tossed onto the rubbish heap.

Remove the things that tempt my eyes with perversity,
    seductively drawing my thoughts away from You.
Still my tongue when it longs
    to share a morsel of gossip
or tell a lie or slander someone.
Silence evil thoughts of getting even,
    spiteful acts, or proud deceit.

How easy it is to look righteous on the outside—
    how difficult to live in purity within.
Help me not to wear Your Holy Spirit like a garment—
    covering up my selfishness and pride.

Cleanse my heart by Your power, God,
    that Your true light may shine forth unhindered.

Every morning silence my sinful yearnings
    and take my hand to walk the day with You.

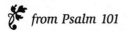 *from Psalm 101*

Moving

"Hear my prayer, O LORD;
    let my cry for help come to You.
Do not hide Your face from me
    when I am in distress.
Turn Your ear to me;
    when I call, answer me quickly."

I have poured my life into this house,
    this neighborhood, this community
    and have put down roots deep into its soil.
I know the streets and corners—
    where the tall trees crowd together
        forming an arch of green in summer,
            of lacy black branches in winter's icy days.
My friends live near enough to see each day,
    and playmates ride their bikes
        to join my children in play.

Now we must leave,
    move to a different place
        with unfamiliar streets and trees and faces.

I do not sleep for all my wondering—
    will my children find new friends at school?
        will they be behind their peers in new classes?
        where will we live?
            where will we go to church?
Doubts crowd my mind, filling it to overflowing.
    And my fears become my food, day after day.

But You, O Lord, are my King forever,
    unchanging and unchangeable,
        understanding and compassionate.

You know these things that hold my heart are temporary.
    Houses and trees, streets, and even friends
        don't last forever.

Perhaps I need this change to loosen my grip
        on passing things
    and to strengthen my heart's grip on You.

Help me, my Father, to rely on Your reliability,
    to remember You belong to neither time nor space.
In You there is a constancy the world cannot provide,
    a love that is eternally secure.

When we must leave the people and places we know,
    remind us that we never leave Your side.
Please travel with us to our destination, Lord,
    and let us serve You in our new home.
Prepare our hearts to find You in each circumstance
    and learn that all things change except Your love.

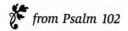 *from Psalm 102*

Prayer to discipline properly

"Praise the LORD, O my soul;
    all my inmost being, praise His holy name.
Praise the LORD, O my soul,
    and forget not all His benefits."

Remind me of Your innumerable mercies to me, Lord,
    especially when I am tempted
        to be too harsh with my children.

I know that sometimes the punishment I mete out
    comes from frustration and anger
        more than from the need to correct behavior.

Bring to mind the way You treat me when I fail
    to meet Your standards.

You forgive my sins and heal my diseases.
    Give me a heart of forgiveness and healing words.

You redeem me from the pit of failure and despair.
    Give me an encouraging manner
        that lifts up my children.

You give me good things so I may be satisfied.
    Give me wisdom to know how
        to give my children hope.

You deal with me in just and righteous ways.
    Give me discernment to choose the correct path.

You make Your ways known to me.
    Help me communicate them clearly
        and lovingly to my children.

You are compassionate and gracious.
    Keep me from embarrassing my children
        or being unfair.

You are slow to anger, abounding in love.
    Help me hold my temper and convey love
        in many different ways.

You do not treat me as my sins deserve.
    Help me give my children second chances,
        extending trust.

You treat me with such love
        because You remember how frail I am.
    Let me recall that these little ones
        aren't finished growing up yet.

You see how quickly my life is gone,
        yet You treasure me.
    My children will grow and leave so quickly,
        help me show them how precious they are.

You are the Lord of heaven and of earth.
    Your kingdom never ends.
    Help me lead my children to praise Your name
        both now and in eternity.

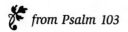 *from Psalm 103*

God is always enough

O God, Your greatness is amazing!
   Light is Your garment,
      and the heavens cannot contain You.
All things are created by You,
   and everything exists at Your command.
Surely You are the God who is enough—
   enough to feed and clothe and satisfy
      all Your creation.

How do I convey that to my children?
   Theirs is the generation of "never enough."
They bombard me with requests for more of everything—
   more money, more clothes, more music,
      more freedom, more time.
Never satisfied, even when receiving what they seek,
   again they set out for more.
And the things they think will bring them joy,
   lose their attraction once they're owned.

Am I that way with You, Father?
   Do I seek things You do not want me to have,
      whining like a petulant child for more and more?
Perhaps my children's dissatisfaction
   is just a mirror of my own—
      begging for more possessions, more appreciation,
      more peace, more control.

Give me a fresh vision of Your abundance
   offered with an open hand
      to all who call You *Lord.*
Let me find deep contentment with all You've given me—
   gifts of Your glorious love.

In the morning, I will sing to You
      praises and songs of thanks
   and meditate on Your goodness as I lie in my bed.
For all that lives draws breath at Your command,
   and nothing good exists without Your power.

Praise the Lord, O my soul.
   Praise the one who always is enough.

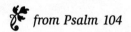 *from Psalm 104*

When a crisis threatens

O Lord, just when I think my life is settling down,
    along comes another crisis.
I'm tired and overwhelmed.
    I'm not sure I can go through another valley.

I look ahead and the way is dark.
    Confusion and uncertainty stand like giants
        in my path.
How can I walk with courage
    when all I feel is fear?
How can I give my children hope
    when all I sense is despair?

Then I hear that still small voice
    whispering in my heart:
        "Don't look ahead, look back."

Look back at times when I was lost,
    and You came looking for me.
Look back at days when panic raged,
    and You brought calm.
Look back when sickness threatened to destroy,
    and You brought healing.
Look back when I was all alone,
    and You took my hand.

Time after time in the past, You rescued me
    and gave me strength to carry on,
        sometimes hour by hour.
There was never a time when You weren't there
    to comfort and defend.
There were no nights so dark Your light was gone.

Remembering all Your faithfulness,
  I raise my eyes again and know Your peace—
    a peace I cannot understand.

"Come here, my children, gather here beside me now
  and let me tell you what the Lord has done.
If He so loved us in the days that went before,
  won't He be faithful now to see us through?"

In their eyes, I see a peace reflected back,
  the peace that only Your dear Son can give.

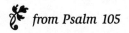 *from Psalm 105*

If a teenager turns from God

O Lord, I give thanks
    for all You have done for our family.
  I recall the children who once were little,
    singing songs to You in choirs and pageants.
How joyfully they skipped to Sunday school
  week after week, memorizing their Bible verses.
At night, kneeling beside their beds, we prayed together,
    blessing relatives faraway
      and kittens curled up in their arms.
They never questioned faith;
  it was as natural as every breath they drew.
God was Father, Jesus their dearest friend,
    and if they thought the Holy Spirit was truly a ghost,
      I smiled and knew You certainly understood.

Have they now, in their adolescent arrogance,
    forgotten all those times of fellowship with You?
They shrug their shoulders at questions of faith,
    grumble when we go to church,
      and find excuses not to pray.

I see them turning away from You
    and long to draw them back,
      but all my arguments are discarded
        as outdated and irrelevant.

Their altar is the video, the CD, the computer,
    pounding messages of other gods
      that draw them to worship electronic images.

Now I bring my prayers to You, O Lord.
    Please work Your healing in their rebellious hearts.

Cause them to turn back and follow You,
    to place their hearts and minds into Your care.
They do not hear my voice when I call them,
    but Yours can cut through the noise
        they use to shut You out.

Have mercy on them,
    gather them once more to kneel before Your throne,
        to worship and adore Your name alone.
May we once more be united in our family time of prayer
    and give thanks and praise You together evermore.

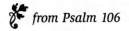 *from Psalm 106*

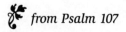

Thanks for God's blessings

"Give thanks to the LORD, for He is good;
  His love endures forever."
You have blessed us in so many ways.
  We have a home and love of children and friends.
You have lifted us to a place where we enjoy
  physical comforts and even some luxuries.
You have crowned us with good health
  and given us pleasant places in which to walk.
In Your mercy, You have not afflicted us with tragedy
  nor have You led us into despair.

O Lord, help us never to forget Your graciousness to us.
Let me teach my children day by day
  that all we have and are comes from You.
Your love is never ending.
  It frees us from fear
    and rescues us from grief.

When the days bringing shadows come
    and storm clouds gather on our family's horizon,
      let us not forget Your benefits and blessings.

Draw us ever closer to You in times of trouble.
  Remove any doubt of Your love
    when circumstance are less than ideal.

Make me an example for my children
  that I may sing to You in both dark and sunny times.
May they learn that life is changeable as the sea,
  and only You are constant through it all.

from Psalm 107

When the family enters God's service

"My heart is steadfast, O God;
　　I will sing and make music with all my soul."
Your love is great—higher than the heavens;
　　Your faithfulness reaches to the skies.

You have called our family to the mission field
　　and charged us to share You with the nations!
More than anything, we want to exalt You, O God,
　　in all we do and say as we minister
　　　　in this faraway place.

But we can do nothing without Your help.
　　In myself I see pockets of doubt,
　　　　fears about my children's health,
　　　　　　their education, their socialization.
To so many of our family and friends,
　　this seems a foolish choice—
　　　　an emotional decision rashly made
　　　　　　without regard to consequences.
How can I explain that consequences
　　are what draw us away—
　　the consequences of a starving child,
　　　　a mother without hope of survival,
　　　　　　a father racked by helplessness.

Focus our eyes on You,
　　the God who owns all peoples and nations.
Go before us, Lord, into the battle.
　　Give us aid against our enemies.
All our strength is nothing without Your hand,
　　and You will bring the victory when it comes.

from Psalm 108

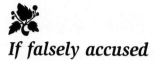

If falsely accused

O God, whom I praise,
    do not remain silent,
        for I have spoken up for right.
Now lying and gossiping people
    seek to destroy my reputation.

Day after day their taunts increase—
    even those I counted as friends turn their backs.
I know You taught Your disciples
    to turn the other cheek, Jesus.
You said to forgive seventy times seven,
    to not repay evil for evil
        but to love my enemies
            and pray for my persecutors.

I'm not doing a good job of praying for them, Lord.
    I want them to suffer as I have suffered,
        to feel the stab of an unjust accusation.
Vengeance and retribution fill my thoughts.
    I imagine all sorts of dreadful consequences
        falling on their heads!

But in my bitterness and anger,
    I only feel more lonely and depressed.
I am a poor and needy child, Father,
    who hasn't learned her lessons well
        for still I feel the sting of hate
            well up within my heart.

I know You want to teach me through this pain.
    Could You give me a glimpse of Your purposes?

Is it that You want my pride to be an offering
poured out for You,
my will melted in this fire
so You can reform it to reflect Yours?

Help me, O Lord my God.
Save me in accordance with Your love.
Let me live the lessons You have taught,
regardless of the cost.
In the end, may it be You, not I, who is lifted up
that Your name may receive praise forevermore.

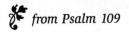 *from Psalm 109*

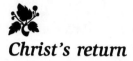

Christ's return

My son asked me the other day,
   "When will Jesus come back, Mom?
      What will happen then?"

The two of us spoke of what it would be like,
   how glorious it will be to see You come
      in the morning,
   to see all darkness flee before Your light.
Your majesty and glory will outshine the dawn;
   Your justice will fall like dew on all nations.

What great confidence Your promises give us, O Lord.
   How wonderful it is to share this hope
      with those I love.
But let me not forget that victory also brings defeat,
   that there are those who will face Your wrath.
Let my joy and anticipation
   not become a selfish attitude
      that judges and prevents others
         from finding truth.
For in that day,
   there will be no rejoicing in others' loss,
      only sad accounting of their fate.

Show me how to teach my children the importance
   of showing others Your face
      so they may also share
         the wonder of Your coming return.

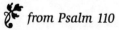 *from Psalm 110*

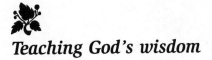

Teaching God's wisdom

I will lift up Your name, Jesus,
    not only in the safety of the sanctuary,
        but in my family and neighborhood too.

We so eagerly seek the right school, the right teacher,
    anxiously inspect each addition to the curriculum.
Are we so concerned with intellectual enlightenment
    that we forget the value of Your wisdom?

My children need to be reminded of Your great works.
    Next to them, the achievements of humanity pale.
There are so many deeds receiving praise today,
    but only Yours are eternally righteous.

Your gracious compassion, undeserved and freely given,
    rescues Your children from helplessness and fear.
You provide an identity, a place of belonging,
    for all who call on Your name.

You are completely trustworthy
    in the midst of a world that doesn't value promises
        and tosses commitment to the winds.

You make it possible for hope to become reality,
    for all who are lost to be found.

The fear of the Lord is truly the beginning of wisdom.
    Let all who follow Your precepts
        find understanding.

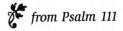 *from Psalm 111*

Praise to God for "chain of mothering"

How independent I was when I first became a mother!
　　How I longed to prove I could do the job
　　　　with a patience and skill my parents never had!
I thought all my ideas were so innovative,
　　my techniques enlightened,
　　　　my insights filled with wisdom.

Now, after mothering for many years, I look back
　　and see how much credit belongs to *my* mother.
My children are blessed
　　because she took the time to mother me.
She was generous with her praise,
　　and with her discipline came love and hope.
Her faithfulness taught me much about commitment;
　　her patience taught me love.
Even in times of darkness,
　　she brought the light of common sense and wit.
She didn't look to me to satisfy her unmet needs
　　or use my personality to fulfill her own.
Her gifts of laughter, listening, open affection,
　　and devotion were given unreservedly,
　　　　day after day.

What kind of mother would I be
　　without my mother's investment of herself in me?
Looking at my children now, I wonder.
　　Will my investment in their character be enough
　　　　to carry them through their parenting days?

Generation after generation
　　the Lord has promised to bless
　　　　if we are faithful to the task
　　　　　　He sets before us every day.

As a mother, make me a strong link in that chain
that stretches through the generations,
joining families from long ago
with families yet to come
so that Your name, O Lord,
is lifted up.

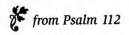 *from Psalm 112*

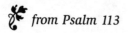

Thanks for children

O Lord, Your name is lifted up,
    honored above all other names.
        From horizon to horizon, You are glorified.

Who is like You, Father?
    Who can even approach Your majesty and power?
Yet in all Your greatness,
    You never forget us.

Gently, You raise us up when we are helpless;
    tenderly You lift us out of our despair.
You allow us to sit at Your feet,
    like well-loved children
        gathered into a father's kind embrace.

Thank You for giving me the desires of my heart,
    for settling me in a pleasant place,
        and for allowing me to gather my children
            into my embrace.
For You know the joy that children bring,
    the filling of the heart to overflowing.

from Psalm 113

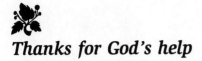

Thanks for God's help

Jesus, when I bring You my impossibilities,
    they become opportunities
        for praise and thanksgiving.

I look at the challenges I face
    with children, job, schedules, house,
        and I see barriers, blockades, frustration.

Yet You show me the way
    to pass through the stormy seas that overwhelm me.
At Your command, the path is cleared,
    priorities clarified through prayer.

Thank You for turning the dry and barren places
    into streams of blessing,
        for demonstrating once more
            that You are the God
                who overcomes all obstacles.

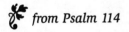 *from Psalm 114*

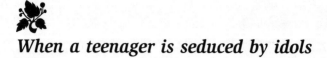

When a teenager is seduced by idols

Lord, show me how to turn my children's eyes
    away from this world's cheap, imitation gods
        toward the precious gold of Your Son.

Fast cars, stylish clothes, the latest electronics—
    these are the gods who bring the blessings
        of teenage acceptance and popularity.
They seduce with promises—
    more friends, more opportunities, more recognition.
But what they deliver is quite different—
    more worries, more expenses,
        more hungering for more.
They are empty, impotent gods,
    yet they wield such power over young minds.
How can Your teachings in the Bible
    compete with polls from magazines,
        high school heroes,
    and ever-changing styles and fads and trends?

Hear my prayer, dear Jesus,
    and open the eyes of my teenagers to Your truth.
Only You are able to satisfy
    our hunger for acceptance.
Only You are powerful enough to fill
    the emptiness when friends betray
        and status disappears.
When our possessions rust and fall apart,
    relationships are lost and laughter ends,
        You alone stand firm from everlasting,
            alive with the power and wisdom
                born of Truth.

 from Psalm 115

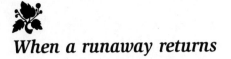

When a runaway returns

"I love the LORD, for He heard my voice;
    He heard my cry for mercy.
Because He turned His ear to me,
    I will call on Him as long as I live."

When our daughter ran away,
    I knew a fear like nothing I had known before.
Horrible scenes crowded every thought,
        and grief squeezed my heart
            with every anguished beat.
There was nowhere to turn, no help from anyone,
        until I turned to You and cried,
            "O Lord, save me!"

You heard my cry, a mother's prayer of pain,
        and in Your gracious compassion,
            You worked a miracle of peace.

Before the lost was found,
        You offered hope and Your protecting love.
Into the darkness of my fear,
        You sent the light of Your Spirit
            to illumine and inspire.

When she walked in the door—
        unharmed, afraid, confused—
            and fell into my arms,
                in that moment I knew the joy
                    of the prodigal's return,
                        felt the throb of a grateful heart.

How can I repay You for Your goodness to me?
What price is enough
    for the blessings You have brought?
I will renew my vows of servanthood,
    lift up Your name to all with praise and thanks,
       demonstrate with actions and with words
         an obedience born of love.
For You have freed me from the chains of grief
    and restored to me the life of my lost child.

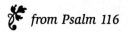 *from Psalm 116*

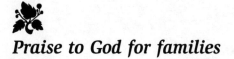

Praise to God for families

Praise the Lord all you families.
Praise His name all you mothers and fathers.
Sing to Him a new song you sons and daughters.

For great is His love toward us.
He has placed us together to demonstrate His love,
to teach us to grow in grace and mercy,
to nurture us one by one.

He will always be faithful to us,
and His love will endure forever.

Praise the Lord.

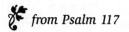 *from Psalm 117*

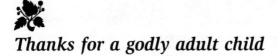

Thanks for a godly adult child

"Give thanks to the LORD for He is good;
      His love endures forever."

As I look at my children—
      young adults now, who have achieved so much
            yet still honor their father and me—
                  I am overwhelmed with gratitude.
Friends say what a good job we did raising them,
      how we must have set such an excellent example,
            but I know the truth.
      You are the one to receive praise, Jesus.

How many times I cried to You in fear!
      I didn't know what to say or do when crises came.
In the midst of the battle, You fought at my side.
      You answered my prayer and brought the victory.
When worries swarmed around me like angry bees,
      You chased them away with Your words of promise.
Many times I felt my back against the wall,
      pressed by conflicting views, and You lifted me up,
            giving me Your strength for the challenge.

The success of my parenting is not mine to claim.
If there is praise to be received,
      let it be placed at Your feet, my Savior.
It was Your grace that granted us children,
      Your power that enabled me to mother them,
            Your Spirit who will guide them onward now.
I will give thanks to You now and always,
      for You are good. Your love endures forever.

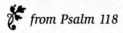 *from Psalm 118*

Teaching the importance of God's Word

Today my young son picked up my Bible
   and carefully opened its well-worn pages.
"Mommy, why do you read this book so much.
   Don't you get tired of the same old stories?"

I laughed at his question and recalled the times
   I found treasures in God's Word.
"Once I would have thought that too," I replied.
   "But come sit here and let me tell you
      why a mother like me and a boy like you
         should spend time reading the Bible.

"God blesses those who live their lives
   according to His Word.
How can you keep your life pure
   unless you know the right way to live?
When we memorize certain verses,
   we can remember them when temptations come.
      God will help us choose to do the right thing.
Sometimes, God's Word tells me I am doing wrong.
   Then I know I need to ask forgiveness.
When I'm sad and feeling all alone,
   God cheers me up as I read how much He loves me.
It's easy to get busy with unimportant things.
   That's when the Bible reminds me
      what is precious and what isn't.
When someone hurts my feelings or makes fun of me,
   God's Word tells me to trust Him
      for He will never treat me unkindly.
When it's dark at night and I feel afraid,
   I remember God is light—

He tells me that in His Word—
then I know I'm safe and don't need to worry.
Even when bad things happen—
like they did to David, Daniel, Peter, Paul—
I remember how God helped them.
Then I know He will help me too.
Other people will not always love God's Word—
some even say the Bible isn't true—
but their words will one day stop.
God's Word goes on forever.

"As you read the Bible and recall what God says,
He gives you wisdom to know the way to go.
He guides you when you are confused
and holds you when you are afraid
and comforts you when you are lonely or sad.
In His Word, God shows the answer
to our greatest problem of sin—
Jesus, our Savior.
It is in God's Son—*the* Word—
that we have a life of hope and joy,
the promise of never ending life with Him."

He reached out his hands and gently touched the Bible.
"Let's read some now, Mommy."
And we did.

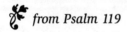 *from Psalm 119*

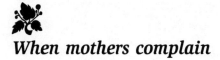

When mothers complain

I call on You, Lord,
  to help me in my distress.

Why can't a group of mothers get together
  without gossiping and back-biting?
Conversations so often veer off into negativism,
  complaining, and griping
    about schools and teachers and coaches,
      about who has what and who said what.

And I am not always an innocent party
  in these conversations.
How easy it is to join in the song of complaint,
  to sing the "Motherhood Blues"!

I know You want my speech to be pure,
  my conversations to encourage and uplift.
Forgive my wayward tongue, Lord,
  and give me words of peace.

from Psalm 120

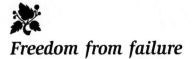

Freedom from failure

Here I am in the pits again, Lord.
    I'm overwhelmed and under-energized.
The house is a mess,
      the kids are demanding more than I have to give,
         my husband doesn't know why I'm upset,
            and I can't see things getting better.

Lift up your eyes.

Are You there, Lord?
    Will You help me?
      If You made heaven and earth,
        maybe You could help me
          make something of the mess I'm in.

He will not let your foot slip nor will He slumber.

You know this is going to be a full-time job.
    I've tried improvement schemes before,
      and my track record isn't very great.

The Lord watches over you day and night.

I'm afraid of losing myself in the battle.
    If I try to be everything to everyone,
      who will I be?
And what if I can't do it?
    What if I fail again and lose my family's love?

The Lord will keep you from all harm—
    He will watch over your life.

I'm going to hold on to You very tightly, Jesus.
    I know I can only succeed
        if You're beside me every step of the way.
Help me to be the woman You designed
    and to fulfill the roles You have given me.

"The LORD will watch over your coming and going
    both now and forevermore."

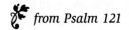 *from Psalm 121*

Praise to God for the church

The church, for me, has always been a secure haven,
    a place for blessed memories,
        joyful fellowship,
            deep, heart-searching worship.

I want my children to grow up feeling this way too.
    I long for them to see their church family
        as an extended family,
            praising God together
                but caring for one another as well.

The older members of the congregation share
        their wisdom,
    the younger ones
        their unbridled enthusiasm.
Together we find common ground in our love for Christ.

Help me foster a love for the church
    in my children's hearts,
        not as a structure or denomination,
          but as a living organism,
        existing to do Your will on earth.

And may each child find within the church
    a place to contribute,
        a place of acceptance,
          a place of peace and grace—
            Your body, Christ, on earth.

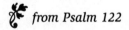 *from Psalm 122*

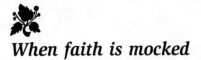

When faith is mocked

I am tired of being stereotyped, Lord,
    just because I believe in You and Your Word.
I am tired of seeing the raised eyebrows,
    the condescending smiles,
        the dismissing glances
            that accompany the label "Christian."

I am proud to bear Your name,
    to be one of Your children,
        yet the contempt of others
            sometimes wears me down.

Focus my eyes on You.
    Show me how to look to You for all I need.
Give me grace to discount the opinions of others
    when it comes to my faith,
        to rest securely in Your arms
            and look into Your face alone.

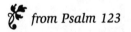 *from Psalm 123*

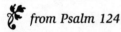

When tragedy is averted

If You had not intervened on our behalf, Lord,
    we would have perished.

There we were, laughing and singing,
    carefree as we traveled down the highway,
        heading for an afternoon at the beach.

Then there was an oncoming car—
    screeching brakes, screaming children,
        shrieking metal, shattering glass,
            tumbling, twisting,
                an upside-down world,
                    then silence,
                        louder than the screams.

The baby cried,
    and I knew I was not dead.
        "Mommy, help me. Mommy can you hear me?"
How good to hear their voices and my own,
    "I'm here. It's going to be all right."

You did not allow us to be torn apart,
    to be swallowed up by this tragedy,
        to be engulfed by grief.

Who can know the mystery of Your grace and mercy, Jesus?
    Why did we all survive and others perish?
You allowed us to escape like birds
    out of the fowler's snare,
        not because of our goodness but Yours alone.

from Psalm 124

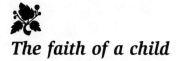

The faith of a child

Today, O Lord, I learned a great lesson in faith.
  I did not learn it from a great preacher,
      a mighty missionary, a philosophy book,
          or a Bible study class.
I learned this great lesson from my little child.

I was worried about an upcoming move,
      about relocating to a different town,
          selling the house, and finding a new home.
My conversations were edged with fear,
      and uncertainty colored all my thoughts.
I hung up the phone after a call from my husband
      and turned to see my little daughter in the doorway.

"What's wrong, Mommy?"
  "Oh nothing, dear, just grown-up things."
"Are they sad things, Mommy?"
  "No, just little problems I need to think about."

She looked relieved, walked over to me,
      and took my hand.
  "My Sunday school teacher says Jesus can solve
      the biggest problems in the whole world,
          so I guess your little problems
              won't give Him any trouble.
                  Can we go to the park now?"

How unshakable is this childlike faith, O Lord,
      how trusting in Your utter goodness.
Help me see Your presence as my child does—
      a protective barrier between us and all our cares.

from Psalm 125

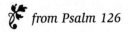

Thanks for a restored marriage

A year ago our marriage looked so hopeless.
    We were two strangers living in the same house,
        eating at the same table,
            listening to the same children,
                going through the motions of a family.

Reluctantly, with resignation and doubts,
    we gave it one more try before calling it quits.
A Christian counselor
    prayed with us, listened to our stories,
        and set about turning us back to You, O Lord.
Little by little,
    sometimes two steps forward and one back,
        coming from our separate places,
            we headed for the cross.

When we met You there,
    You healed us individually and as a couple.
You gave us life as we had never known it,
    freed us from the captivity of our own selfishness,
        fulfilled our dreams of unity and love.
Laughter once more filled our home,
    and thankfulness became our song.
Surely, we said, the Lord has done great things for us.
We went out weeping and empty,
    and You brought us back full of blessing.

We will praise Your name forever,
    singing songs of joy to You.

from Psalm 126

Thanks for God's steadfastness

Unless You, O Lord, are our foundation,
    our family will flounder and our home collapse.
Unless You watch over us, O Lord,
    we are vulnerable to every storm of life.

What good will it do me to be a diligent mother,
    doing all the little things mothers do—
        cooking, cleaning, carpooling, cajoling—
            if I lie awake nights worrying
                because I have not trusted You to guide us?

You have given us these sons and daughters
    and blessed us with the means to support them.
You have rewarded us with challenges that bring growth
    as we seek courage and Your wisdom
        to parent in a godly way.

I thank and praise You
    for Your promises to walk with us constantly,
        to fulfill Your Word faithfully,
            and to hold us in Your hand tenderly
            as we travel this road together.

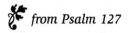 *from Psalm 127*

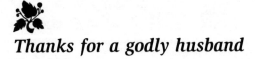

Thanks for a godly husband

I thank You, Father, for giving me a faithful husband.
   In his business dealings, he demonstrates integrity,
      and he is trustworthy in all his relationships.

Not only is he successful in his profession,
   but he works hard to nurture our marriage as well.
He treats me with respect and kindness,
   demonstrating his love in innumerable ways.

He takes time to listen to each child,
   to laugh and play with them
      as well as teach and train them.
Even when he is tired, he is gentle,
   hearing behind their words a hidden fear or hurt.

Bless this man who is my lover and my friend.
   Give him grace to continue when he is weary.
Help me to encourage and affirm him
   as he strives to be a godly husband and father.
May he enjoy a long and fruitful life
   filled with the love of family and friends.

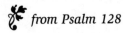 *from Psalm 128*

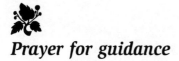

Prayer for guidance

Today I learned I am to be a mother, Lord,
    and my joy and wonder mingle with a breathless fear.
For I did not know my mother.
    She was a stranger to me
        as I grew up in a string of foster homes.
I cannot recall a mother's tender touch,
    the strong security of knowing,
        "Mother will understand."

How can I model something I have never learned?
    My memories are distant, troubling clouds
        in the sky of my childhood.

I long to be for this little one who grows within me
    the kind of mother I longed to have.

Will You cut me free from the cords of my memories
    and see that they do not overwhelm me?

If you will walk before me, Lord,
    I know Your love will guide me day by day.
Together, You and I will raise this little one
    within the sweet security of Your grace.

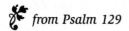 *from Psalm 129*

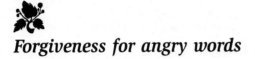

Forgiveness for angry words

"Out of the depths I cry to You, O LORD,
  O Lord, hear my voice.
Let Your ears be attentive to my cry for mercy."

When I returned home and found the house a mess,
  I lost my temper and shouted out in frustration.
Like an angry tide welling up inside,
    my words piled up until they spilled over
      in bitterness and sarcasm,
          drowning my children in their flood.

How many times have I come to You for forgiveness?
  If You kept a record of my sins,
    I would be without hope.

I teach and preach Your principles to my children,
  then in one moment of fury,
    erase the lessons with my cutting words.

Be merciful to me, O Father.
  My soul waits for Your healing touch once more.
Without Your help, I cannot hope to conquer
    this habitual rage.
  Without Your Spirit's leading, I am lost.

Redeem me from my own selfish temperament
  that urges me to lash out when I should be calm.
Replace it with Your peace and gentleness,
  with words of correction that help instead of harm.
Restore our home to harmony through Your strong mercy
  that we may grow together in Your name.

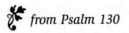 *from Psalm 130*

Childlike dependence on Christ

My heart is not proud, O Lord,
    my eyes do not look down on those with other callings.
I do not concern myself with great matters
    or things too complicated and technical for me.

I am a mother.

I will be still in Your arms, Jesus,
    and learn again to be a child in Your kingdom,
        totally dependent on Your loving care.

I am a mother.

My task is both simple and mighty.
    My hope of success lies with You alone.

Help me now and forevermore,
    my Lord and my Savior.

from Psalm 131

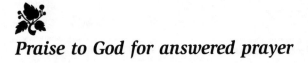

Praise to God for answered prayer

O Lord, You are so faithful to remember Your children.

Year after year, I raised this child to You in prayer
    and asked You to draw her gently to Yourself.
Many were the sleepless nights
    when I cried to You on her behalf.
Days seemed endless as she continued
    on a downward path.
Yet You heard my prayers,
    and in Your perfect time, brought her back.
I thank You for not rejecting her,
    for not forgetting her in her wandering years.

I have claimed Your promises
    and have seen Your fulfillment.
You truly are the God who seeks and saves the lost,
    going to the ends of the earth to rescue them.
I praise Your loving-kindness and Your grace
    that gives us what we never could deserve.
For You have chosen each of us,
    have desired us to belong to Your family,
        have blessed us with abundance
    and clothed us with salvation's gleaming robe.

I will sing a song of joy before Your throne, Lord,
    and lift Your name in praises to the heavens.

Blessed be the God who answers mothers' prayers
    and rescues children from the tempter's grip.

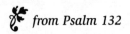 *from Psalm 132*

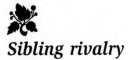

Sibling rivalry

How good and pleasant it is
    when brothers live together in unity!

And how utterly frustrating when they do not!

Lord, I'm ready to lose my mind with these boys.
    What one has, the other wants—
        until he has it, then he loses interest.
    What one says, the other contradicts—
        and then an argument ensues.
My days are filled with refereeing battles—
    Yes you did. *Did not!*
        Did too. *No, I didn't!*
            Give it here. *No, it's mine!*
            Don't you dare! *MOM!!*

Only You can bring peace from all this chaos.
    Only You can show me how to cope.
Please pour the soothing oil of Your Holy Spirit
    over the stormy sea of sibling rivalry, Lord.
        Show my sons the rich and endless blessings
        of a brother's love.

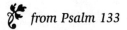 *from Psalm 133*

Praise to God for nursery workers

Lord Jesus, I praise You
     for Your special servants.
  I thank You for the women
    who work in the church nursery.
Week after week, they greet my little one in Your name.
  They show her through gentle hands,
    soft voices, and loving smiles
      that Your house is a happy place.

How seldom they are appreciated for their dedication,
  working in the shadows,
    even when the pastor and choir and others
     are recognized.

Because of them, I can enjoy quiet worship,
  knowing my daughter is well cared for.
I can draw strength from Your Word and fellowship,
  becoming better equipped to be a godly mother.

Bless these dear ones and give them added grace
  as they work for You in Your house.

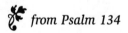 *from Psalm 134*

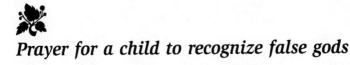

Prayer for a child to recognize false gods

Praise the Lord, all you servants of the Lord,
    Praise the Lord for the Lord is good.

You are great and mighty, O Lord,
        greater than all gods,
    yet Your creation does not call You great
        and finds other gods to take Your place.

I have taught my children
    that You do what pleases You, Lord,
        bringing sun and rain, thunder and wind
            upon the seas.

But the world mocks You, Father,
    calling Your Word a book of myths,
        the deeds of Moses and Joshua legends.
They would reduce Your Son to the status of a sage,
    a gifted philosopher
        with a charismatic personality.

Grant my children strength to stand
    against the tide of public opinion
        in this age of so-called enlightenment
    when Christian faith is mocked as whimsical
        and idolatry elevated as truth.

You have given us wondrous creativity,
    but gods made of microchips and laser beams
        cannot hear my daughter's cry
            or see my son's pain.

Flashing graphics and interactive intelligence
    do not seek the lost
        nor answer sinners' prayers.

Help my children see their culture realistically
    and understand the clear line
        between Creator and creation.

And Lord, give me grace to model
    with certain faith and a consistent life
        the joy of knowing You as a constant reality.

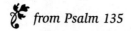 *from Psalm 135*

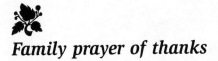

Family prayer of thanks

We join our hands in this family circle, Lord,
    and raise our voices in thanks to You.
Because of Your great love, we know the love
    of parent, child, brother, sister.

You have done great wonders in the world,
    yet You hear the prayers of each of us,
        small as we are.

Your understanding is beyond our imagination,
    but You care enough to listen to us,
        and You understand our hurts and fears.

Your hand created the heavens, the stars, the moon,
    and Your power keeps them in their places,
        yet You still have time to touch our lives.

When our enemies threaten us,
    when our selfish natures lead us into sin,
        You are there to shield and guide us back to You.

When we are hungry or tired or lonely,
    you provide us with food or rest or comfort.

You have even provided a wonderful future for us,
    a future free from fear or pain or worry
        where we will live with You forever,
            together in the oneness of Your love.

We give thanks to You, the God of heaven,
    our Abba whose love endures forever.

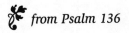 *from Psalm 136*

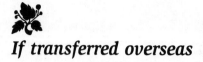

If transferred overseas

Lord, we've been transferred to a foreign land,
 and all we can think of is the home we've left.

It seemed exciting at first.
I read books to our children about our new location
 looking at the pictures of strange new places
  with unfamiliar names.
It was fun creating dinners
 featuring exotic flavors and textures
  in anticipation of our wonderful adventure.

Belongings were packed,
 good-byes were said,
  planes were caught,
   and now we're here—
    in a new house,
     in a new land,
      feeling lost and alone.
Unfamiliar faces greet me on the streets,
 and undecipherable words pound my ears.
My children feel out of place,
 and I am just as unsettled as they.

Teach me to sing Your songs of joy again, O Lord.
 Lead me to discover here a fellowship of believers.
  Show me the way to help my family settle in.
   Give me the grace to take things day by day.

I believe Your will has brought us here, dear Father,
 so will You hold my hand as I find my way?

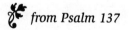 *from Psalm 137*

When speaking about God in a hostile setting

I will praise You, O Lord, with all my heart.
    Before those who reject You,
        I will tell of Your greatness.
For You have never rejected me
    but have always demonstrated
        Your love and faithfulness.

Today I have been asked to speak
        at my children's school, Lord,
    and tell why I think they should permit
        Your name to be mentioned at graduation.
It seems such a small thing, yet I am fearful.
    Give me the courage of my commitment
        mixed with the gentleness of Your Son
            as I present this case.
Make my words bold—strengthened by Your Spirit—
    clear and logical, not frenzied and emotional.

May others be encouraged, not embittered, by my remarks.
    Create a sense of reconciliation in all of us.
It does no good for the cause to be won
    if hearts are hardened
        and people are divided by anger.

As I walk through this trouble, preserve me.
    As I speak, let my words be empty of selfish pride.
Lord, please fulfill Your purpose in this situation
    that Your love will be seen
        and Your works made known.

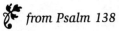 *from Psalm 138*

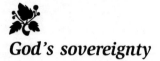

God's sovereignty

O Lord, You have searched me and You know me.
　　What a comfort to know
　　　　You understand everything about me.
When I feel misunderstood by my husband
　　and misjudged by my children,
　　　　I take heart in the knowledge of Your
　　　　　　complete awareness of every aspect
　　　　　　　　of my personality.

You not only know me,
　　but You also direct and guide me
　　　　with a love too wonderful to comprehend.
Never am I alone
　　or even far from You.
Your presence surrounds and fills me
　　as surely as the air I breathe.
When I am distressed and confused,
　　Your light guides me out of my darkness.
I do not need to explain myself to You
　　for You created me and understand my every thought.
Before I was born,
　　You attended to the details
　　　　of both my body and my soul,
　　weaving me together in Your perfect pattern.

How can I even attempt to understand
　　the wonder of Your gracious love, Lord?
For in the midst of my fallenness,
　　You still make Yourself known to me,
　　　　touching my inmost thoughts
　　　　　　with the tenderness of Your Spirit.

How I desire to fulfill Your plans for me—
　　to be the wife, mother, sister, friend
　　　　You intended from the beginning.
Help me resist destructive thought patterns—
　　enemies of my peace that seek to steal
　　　　Your presence from my heart.
Search me, try me, examine my heart
　　　　with Your searing truth
　　and purge the anxiety that makes me
　　　　weak and empty.
Lead me, instead, in the way of Your Son,
　　the way that is everlasting.

from Psalm 139

When there's neighborhood trouble

Rescue me, O Lord, from the influence
    of those who would draw me into evil plots
        and controversies.
Let me be an influence for peace and righteousness,
    not anger and vengeance.

How quickly an affront becomes a cause
    when someone's "rights" are trampled.
It started as a simple problem,
    and now the neighborhood is divided into camps.
The children, hearing angry parents,
    rush to take up the fight.
And self-righteousness pours into the streets
    through furious exchanges and unveiled threats.

I want my children to see an example
    of godly behavior in all this discord,
        but I see their excitement
            in the escalating tensions.

Each day is a new chapter in the feuding,
    fueled by real and imaginary insights
        tossed out like last night's trash.

Make our family a force for peace and reconciliation.
May Your justice fall like cooling rain
    on over-heated tempers.
And through this difficult experience,
    may individuals and families
        become neighbors once again,
            united in a common goal of peace.

 from Psalm 140

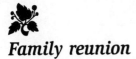

Family reunion

O Lord, I call to You.
>Hear my voice as I pray.

It's time for the family reunion again,
>and I want it to be healing and restorative.

Set a guard over my mouth, O Lord.
>Keep watch over the door of my lips.

Make me a good listener.
>Keep me from taking sides in old disputes.

Give me a clarity of vision from Your Spirit
>to see points of reconciliation, not division.

I don't want to be a willing participant
>in conversations of family gossip and rumor,
>>dredging up old hurts,
>>>reopening old wounds.

Show me how to accept each person as he or she is
>instead of looking for ulterior motives
>>or hidden agendas.

Help me accept my shortcomings with grace and wit,
>willing to claim my part in the family mosaic.

I pray for a gathering that focuses on You, Lord,
>and on the strong foundation of family love.

May our diversities be appreciated
>for the richness they represent
>>and our common bonds be found in faith.

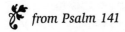 *from Psalm 141*

The frenzy of motherhood

"I cry aloud to the LORD;
    I lift up my voice to the LORD for mercy.
I pour out my complaint before Him;
    before Him I tell my trouble."

I am overwhelmed with mothering, Lord.
    I have lost my direction
        in the midst of everyday responsibilities.
With three children under four years of age,
    I have no time to think, to plan, to regroup.
My day is filled with meals and laundry,
    with potty-training, diapers, and messes.
Is this what mothering is supposed to be?

I long to have a quiet time
    to be alone with You, Jesus.
But there are no quiet moments in my day,
        and at night I am too exhausted
        to whisper more than a hurried prayer for strength.

I look around and see other mothers
    who seem to have it all together,
        masters at balancing children and chores.
My husband is busy with his work,
    and I don't want to weigh him down with my needs.

Only You can offer me relief
    and show the way to freedom from this frenzy.
Rescue me from the enemies of my peace,
    the doubts that chase my confidence away.

I long to praise Your name with a song once more,
to raise my voice in a prayer of joy.

Adjust my focus to Your perspective, not mine,
Set my course according to Your will.

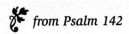 *from Psalm 142*

Prayer for release from memories

"O LORD, hear my prayer,
　　listen to my cry for mercy;
　　　　in Your faithfulness and righteousness
　　　　　　come to my relief."

The memories of my past are like enemies,
　　pursuing me relentlessly and crushing my spirit.
They surround me with darkness,
　　and I am exhausted from the effort of forgetting.

I know that You are able, Lord,
　　to release me from their bitter grip
　　　　and free me from their power to enslave.
So I lift my hands to You in prayer,
　　like a parched woman begs for water in the desert,
　　　　seeking the relief only You can give.
Renew my mind with Your unfailing love
　　for I have put my trust in You.
Show me new patterns of thought and behavior
　　so my children are not burdened
　　　　with the damage of my broken past.

You are my God, and I desire to follow You,
　　responding to Your Spirit daily
　　　　as He leads me along the path of faith.

Heal and restore me,
　　not because I deserve it or could earn it,
　　　　but because of Your unfailing love.
Direct me in the way I should go
　　that I may serve You faithfully forever.

from Psalm 143

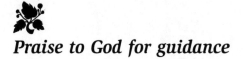

Praise to God for guidance

Praise to You, O Lord, my Rock,
>for You equip me with all I need
>>to face the challenges of mothering.

You are not only the God of the universe,
>but a very personal Father, giving me guidance,
>>and protection as I seek to train my children.

Why is it that You care about me,
>an unremarkable woman with two young children?
Among the millions of families in the world,
>who are we that You should love and care for us
>>with such personal and individual attention?

You are able to split mountains and part seas,
>yet You give me guidance when I am perplexed
>>about equitably dividing my time and attention
>>>so each child feels special.
You are able to direct nations and deliver captives,
>and still You grant me Your wisdom
>>when I face difficult decisions in our family.
You grant victory to kings and generals
>but take the time to assist me
>>when disputes set sister against brother,
>>>parent at odds with child.
Your discerning Spirit
>discloses lies and deceit
>>so that appropriate discipline is applied
>>>and we can live again in harmony.

I thank You, Lord, for Your mercy
 that allows me to nurture my son and daughter
  in ways that bring blessings as they grow.
May they always seek to follow You
 and grow strong in body and spirit
  to be a blessing to their world,
   bringing glory to Your name.

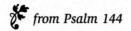 *from Psalm 144*

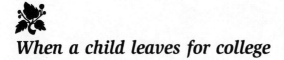

When a child leaves for college

As you leave for college, my child,
    let me send with you this psalm of praise
        that you might always recall
            the one whose faithfulness
                brought you here and will lead you on.

The Lord is great with a greatness You cannot fathom.
    His glory and majesty are awesome,
        creating and sustaining the universe
            from the largest galaxy
                to the smallest atomic particle.
Yet in all His greatness, in the midst of His majesty,
    He chooses to be your dearest friend,
        to touch your life in small and mighty ways.

When you have made a mess of things
    and you feel there are no solutions,
        the Lord is compassionate and slow to anger.
His love is rich and deep and will restore you.

When your friends have broken their promises
        or have betrayed your trust and you are alone,
    the Lord maintains His truth,
        honoring His promise
            to neither forsake nor leave you.

When you are hungry for companionship,
    thirsty for a relationship that satisfies your soul,
        the Lord offers His fellowship,
            fulfilling your deepest needs.

When you are lonely and need someone to talk to,
 the Lord is near and hears your every prayer.
When you are lost and without direction,
 the Lord will guide your feet
  in the way you should go.

I cannot walk beside you as you leave our home
 to find the future God has planned for you,
  but I can assure you with this truth:
The Lord is always faithful to His own
 and loving toward all He has made.

Praise His holy name now and forever.

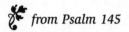 *from Psalm 145*

A widowed mother's prayer

"Praise the LORD, O my soul.
    I will praise the LORD all my life.
    I will sing praise to my God as long as I live."

You've taught me some difficult lessons
    over the years, Lord.
    And perhaps the most painful
        began the year my husband died,
            leaving me a widow with three children.

How I loved him,
    even teasingly calling him my "Prince."
        He was the fulfillment of my dreams.
His faith was strong, his character true,
    and I depended on him for support
        in my weaker moments.
He was there for me—
    listening, caring, holding, encouraging—
        always, he was there.
Then in one swift moment,
    he was gone—and with him, my foundation.
All my hopes, dreams, plans
    were shattered, empty, nothing.
And I was left without the one I had always counted on,
    with three children counting on me.

We had some rough times, You and I, didn't we, Lord?
Until the day I finally looked to You
    instead of my memories.

You showed me gently, tenderly,
    that You made everything
        and were greater than all You created,
           greater than all my grief.
You assured me constantly, repeatedly,
    that You are everlasting,
        never would You leave me,
           never would You abandon my children.
You took my hand when I couldn't see the way,
    and day after day You fed us
        with Your sustaining Word.
In the darkness, You showed us Your light;
    in our fear, Your peace;
        in our emptiness, Your fulfillment.
You truly sustain the fatherless and the widow,
    providing the foundation for our lives
        that will never be shaken
           by life or death.

How I praise You for Your sustaining love
    showered upon us in an abundance we never imagined.
May You reign in our family forever
    as Lord and King.

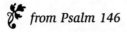 *from Psalm 146*

Praise and thanks to God

How can I ever praise You enough
    for all Your love to me, Jesus?
You are the God who spoke to Abraham and to Moses,
    yet You speak to me, a young mother.
You parted the sea and gathered Your people,
    yet You see my wounded spirit
        and mend my child's broken heart.
You created and named each star in the heavens,
    yet You know my name
        and understand my every thought.

I sing to You with thanksgiving
    for Your love that has no limit.
Your great power and majesty
    stretch across the sky,
        bringing sun and rain,
            giving life to all things.
Despite the glory of the world,
    You choose to delight in us, Your children—
        we who have placed our trust in You.

Thank You for Your blessings:
    security of the soul, peace of the heart,
        satisfaction of the spirit.
How can these compare with the gifts the world offers?

Only You have power over all things,
    speaking life and death with every word.
Yet in Your strength, Your gentleness has called us,
    and tenderly You lead us day by day.

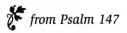 *from Psalm 147*

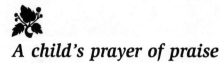

A child's prayer of praise

Praise the Lord from the heavens,
    praise Him from the heights above.
Praise the Lord, all you angels,
    praise Him for His endless love.

Praise the Lord for the sunlight,
    shining in the sky all day.
Praise the Lord for the starlight,
    gently falling as I pray.

Praise the Lord, you gentle raindrops,
    sending water on the ground.
Praise the Lord, you quiet snowflakes,
    spread your blanket all around.

Praise the Lord, you mighty mountain,
    sing His songs, you flashing sea.
Praise the Lord, great wind and thunder,
    sigh His name, you bending tree.

Praise the Lord, all you wild creatures,
    roaring lions, birds so small.
Praise the Lord with all your voices,
    praise His glory, one and all.

Praise the Lord, dear friends and neighbors,
    mommies, daddies, brothers too.
Praise the Lord for He is mighty,
    yet He still loves me and you.

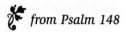 *from Psalm 148*

Teaching a child about the joy of the Lord

O Lord, let me give my children
    a picture of You that causes them to rejoice.

So often it is easy to make faith a matter of rules,
    of rights and wrongs, choices and consequences.

In my efforts to be an effective mother,
    remind me of the sheer joy of praise,
        the delightful dance of worship,
            the songs of wonder at Your grace.

Guide my children to a deep contentment
        in Your blessings,
    an inner fountain that cannot be kept still
        but bubbles forth in praise and thankfulness.

The power of Your truth is not in threats or fear
    but in Your faithfulness day by day
        to those who call You Abba.

This is the glory I want to share with my children:
    the knowledge that in You is fullness of joy.

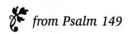 *from Psalm 149*

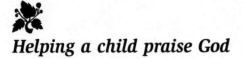

Helping a child praise God

O my children, if you learn nothing else,
    learn to praise the Lord.

Learn to praise Him with all the strength you have,
    to honor His name in actions and in words.

When you see the world around you,
    praise Him for His mighty power
        that created everything.

When you play an instrument or sing a song,
    praise Him for the gift of music.

When you walk or run or dance,
    praise Him for the gift of your body,
        created by Him to bring glory to His name.

When you rise or rest,
    when you sit or stand,
        with every breath
            give praise to the Lord, your God.

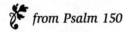 *from Psalm 150*